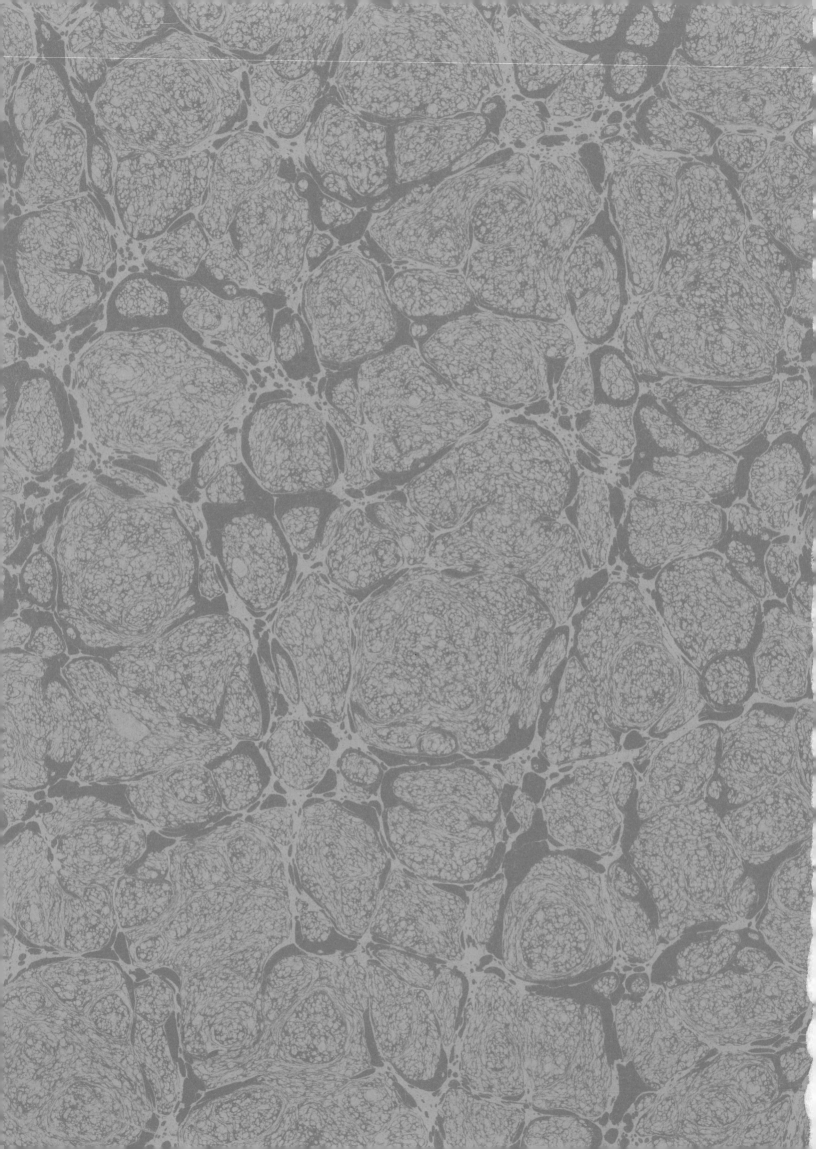

Historic
New York

Architectural Journeys in the Empire State

*This book is dedicated to
Henry McCartney,
whose initiative, assistance, and support
made it possible.*

The English garden and pond at Westbury House, Old Westbury, Long Island.

Montauk Point Lighthouse, Long Island.

Historic New York

Architectural Journeys in the Empire State

PHOTOGRAPHY

ANDY OLENICK

[signature]

TEXT

RICHARD O. REISEM

[signature]

DESIGN

Lynn Buehlman *Design*

COORDINATOR

Sherri Olenick

PRODUCTION

Gary R. Clark

Published by
LANDMARK SOCIETY OF WESTERN NEW YORK, INC.
in conjunction with
PRESERVATION LEAGUE OF NEW YORK STATE
and
NEW YORK STATE COUNCIL ON THE ARTS,
with support provided by
MARGARET L. WENDT FOUNDATION
and
FURTHERMORE,
the publication program of the J. M. Kaplan Fund

First published in the United States of America in 2006
by the Landmark Society of Western New York, Inc.
Rochester, New York 14608-2204

© 2006 Photographs by Andy Olenick
© 2006 Text by Richard O. Reisem

Library of Congress Control Number: 20066921566
ISBN: 0-9763910-2-3

Funded in part by the
New York State Council on the Arts

Printed in the USA by
Canfield & Tack, Inc.
Rochester, New York 14608-2802

Distributed by
Syracuse University Press

CONTENTS

New York State Contributions To American Architecture

*N̲ew York State, through several centuries, made enormous contributions to America's architec-
tural scene. From the works of the Iroquois Indian Nations, through Dutch Colonial and
French Huguenot settlements of the 1600s, and onward to the making of the Empire State after the
construction of the Erie Canal and beyond, New York has contributed diverse, distinctive, and
innovative architecture to the country. Here are some of the unique architectural styles, as well as
the oldest, the largest, the firsts, the inventions, the innovators, and the architectural features that
are the precious contributions to the field of architecture from the State of New York.*

Seneca Indian longhouse in Ganondagan.

1600s

• Unique to New York State is the longhouse of the Iroquois Confederacy. Ganondagan State
Historical Site in Ontario County is the location of a major 17th-century Seneca Indian farming
village comprised of several longhouses and a palisaded granary. The Seneca people refer to
Ganondagan as the "Town of Peace" and believe that the Mother of Nations is buried there. In
1687, the French destroyed the village during a campaign aimed at eliminating the Seneca nation.
Today, Ganondagan contains a reconstructed longhouse and was designated a National Historic
Landmark in 1964. Longhouses are 50 to 200 feet in length, 20 feet wide, and 20 feet high. Their
construction involved a framework of wooden poles tied together and covered with bark. They
were surrounded by fences consisting of long poles stuck close together into the ground. The
fences provided protection in time of war, kept out wolves and other animals, and were a barrier
to winter winds. From 15 to 20 families lived in the bigger longhouses—each family having its
own private section in the open interior. Fires were spaced along the center of the longhouse,
and smoke escaped through holes in the roof. The centrally located fires were shared by several
families for cooking and warmth. Raised wooden platforms provided seating and sleeping
surfaces.

*Dutch steep roofs keep
out wind-driven rain.*

• From 1609 to 1664, New York was a Dutch colony called New Netherland.
It was settled by the Dutch who naturally built structures in Dutch style.
Dutch houses had steeper roofs than English houses, the reason being that
the wind in the Netherlands was stronger than in England, and wind-driven
rain penetrated under wooden shingles on low-pitched roofs, causing them to
leak. Even after tile replaced wood on Dutch roofs, the steep pitch was
retained. Since land was expensive in the Netherlands, houses tended to
make full use of it by having narrow first floors with overhanging upper
floors. Typical Dutch houses also had their gable ends facing the street, which
was not the case with English houses. Also, Dutch houses tended to have fewer but larger rooms
than those in England, and chimneys, rather than being placed at the end walls, were often more
centrally positioned in order to provide fireplaces on both sides of a chimney,
thereby heating two rooms instead of one. The most Dutch-looking city in New
York is Albany, with its famous avenues of attached row houses.

• The village of New Paltz was founded in 1678 by a Protestant sect in France
called Huguenots. Here and elsewhere in the Hudson and Mohawk river valleys
Huguenots built their distinctive structures. The Catskill Mountains in New Paltz
provided limestone and wood for building a unique street of houses and a
French church on Huguenot Street, the oldest street in America with its original
buildings.

French Huguenot house in New Paltz.

First octagonal room, Morris-Jumel Mansion.

• The Morris-Jumel Mansion in New York City was a particularly innovative structure when it was built in 1765. The early Federal style house has a two-story portico with a triangular pediment, inventive at the time. Also, the interior has the country's first octagonal room.

• Shakers arrived in New York in 1774, their first settlement was in Watervliet. They established a 3,000-acre settlement in Colonie. Their first meeting house was a gambrel-roofed building built in 1791. Like their dress and furniture, Shaker buildings were austere and durable, models of simplicity and utility. Most of their buildings were fairly large, usually three stories, with symmetrically placed windows.

Lincoln Mineral Baths, Saratoga Springs.

• New York State is famous for its mineral spas, the most popular of which is Saratoga Springs, where General George Washington and hundreds of thousands of visitors since have enjoyed the naturally carbonated spring water. Lincoln Mineral Baths, the oldest spa in the city, was built in 1911 and replaced in 1930 with a white marble structure that is the largest mineral-bath building in the world capable of providing 4,500 baths a day. Other celebrated historic mineral spas in New York State include Sharon Springs and Clifton Springs.

Stepped-peak gable invented in Waterford.

• Waterford was laid out as a village in 1784 and became the center for a new type of gable as houses and stables were built on the grid of streets. The brick end walls of both houses and stables were topped by an innovation called the Waterford gable. It created end walls with a stepped peak instead of the usual slanted top that followed the roof pitch.

• The first architecturally designed college campus in America is Union College in Schenectady, designed by the French architect, J. J. Ramee in 1814.

• A major construction problem facing the Erie Canal builders was how to mortar the joints in the stones of locks and aqueducts with a cement that would not slack, that is, dissolve and weaken when exposed to water. Dr. Andrew Barto proposed a limestone found in Chittenango, New York. He demonstrated the material to canal engineer Canvass White by forming a ball of moist cement and placing it in a pail of water overnight. The next day, the ball was firm enough to roll across the floor without disintegrating. White perfected the product for canal use, making stone locks and aqueducts possible for the first time in American history.

Nott Memorial at Union College.

• Little Falls, New York, claimed the deepest canal lock (40.5 feet) and the longest stone-arch aqueduct in the world (1,184 feet) when the Erie Canal was built between 1817 and 1825. The world's second-longest stone-arch bridge was the Richmond Aqueduct crossing the wide Seneca River in the Montezuma Swamp. Its 31 arches stretched across 1,137 feet of water. For comparison, the Eisenhower lock (1959), Massena, New York, on the St. Lawrence Seaway is 30 feet deep.

• Cobblestone architecture was invented in western New York. It was a construction technique of building sturdy structures from rubble stone faced with small rounded stones laid in horizontal rows and held in place by lime-based mortar. When the Erie Canal was completed in 1825, canal masons (mostly immigrants from Europe) needed work. They noticed that farmers, in clearing their fields, collected piles of rounded stones just sitting in unused mounds. The smooth stones were created by glacier and lake movement, and when the

Cobblestone buildings invented in New York.

glaciers retreated 14,000 years ago and Lake Ontario's shoreline receded by several miles, the stones were left spotting the fields that farmers wanted to till. The unemployed masons offered their services to construct buildings that could be decorated with stones sorted by desired shape, color, and size. To be classified as a cobblestone, the stone must fit in a person's hand. Hundreds of cobblestone houses, churches, and schools (about 500 still standing) were built in the middle of the 19th century, and 90 percent of all the cobblestone structures in America are located within a 60-mile radius of Rochester, New York.

Grain elevators invented in Buffalo.

• In 1842, Joseph Dart invented the grain elevator in Buffalo. He attached buckets to a vertical belt that was powered by steam. The buckets scooped up grain in the boats and dropped it into tall grain elevators. Today, Buffalo has the most outstanding collection of grain elevators in America and is still the largest grain-milling center, which includes flour for eastern domestic and commercial baking and cereals like Cheerios and Wheaties.

• James Bogardus (1800-1874), a New York architect/engineer, erected the first cast-iron building in America. The iron elements of the building were manufactured in 1848 at Bogardus' own New York City factory. It was the first structure with self-supporting, multistoried exterior walls of iron. Erected in lower Manhattan, the four-story building had street façades of self-supporting cast iron, which consisted of many copies of just a few manufactured pieces, including Doric style columns, wall panels, lintels, sills, and decorative ornaments. During the last half of the 19th century, the spread of cast-iron architecture was tremendous, especially in Rochester and New York City where the SoHo Cast Iron Historic District alone has 139 iron-fronted buildings.

1848 Roebling Aqueduct in Highland.

• The first wire-suspension bridge in the world that is still in operation is the Roebling Aqueduct, Delaware and Hudson Canal, in Highland, New York. It was built in 1848.

• Orson Squire Fowler of Fishkill, New York, inspired a building boom of octagonal houses by publishing a book in 1848 called "A Home for All: the Octagon Mode of Building." An eight-sided house was more than an architectural invention to Fowler. He praised it as a means to a healthier lifestyle, because octagon houses, he argued, are better ventilated through the required cupola and admit more daylight. More than 1,000 octagon houses were built in America between 1850 and 1860. His own octagon home in Fishkill had 60 rooms.

Private home in Chautauqua Institution.

• The Chautauqua Institution started as a religious summer retreat in 1874 and expanded into a 750-acre Victorian village with private and public buildings, as well as facilities for programs in art, music, politics, religion, education, and science. The entire village is a National Historic Landmark, cited for being a remarkable architectural phenomenon. Similarly, Thousand Island Park on Wellesley Island in the St. Lawrence River was started in 1875 as a Methodist summer community and now is a 145-acre settlement of some 320 private cottages in Gothic Revival, Queen Anne, Eastlake, Stick, Shingle, and Bungalow style architecture.

Adirondack architecture at Camp Sagamore.

• The distinctive style of Adirondack architecture and furniture was started by William West Durant (1850-1934) whose first venture into architectural design was Camp Pine Knot built in 1879. He combined the rustic qualities of Adirondack log cabins with the decorative gracefulness and long, low lines of Swiss chalets that he had admired on a trip to Switzerland. Thus began the Adirondack style, copied and embellished ever since throughout the region of upstate New York. Durant's masterpiece was Camp Sagamore, which in 1901 he sold to Alfred Gwynne Vanderbilt, the wealthiest man in America.

• The architectural partnership of Charles Follen McKim, William Rutherford Mead, and Stanford White from 1879 to 1909 designed some of the most important buildings in U.S. architectural history. During these 30 years, McKim, Mead & White was the leading architectural firm in America. They designed buildings influenced by Classical and Renaissance models and established a neoclassical revival in the country. The firm completed almost 1,000 major commissions, including in New York City alone such significant structures as Pennsylvania Station, Pierpont Morgan Library, New York University, Columbia University, old Madison Square Garden, Century Association, University Club, Metropolitan Club, Harvard Club, Bowery Savings Bank, Madison Square Presbyterian Church, and Washington Memorial Arch.

• The Brooklyn Bridge was the first great suspension bridge in the world. The bridge connects Manhattan to Brooklyn. When it opened in 1883, after 13 years of construction, the bridge was hailed as an engineering marvel.

First great suspension bridge, Brooklyn.

• No other American artist is more closely associated with Art Nouveau decoration in the U.S. than Louis Comfort Tiffany (1848-1933). His Tiffany Studios in New York City, founded in 1885, created stained-glass windows, glass and silver chandeliers, metalwork, stonework, and often, complete interior designs for countless buildings, some of them represented in this book.

• Elbert Hubbard (1856-1915) went to England in 1894 and visited William Morris' Arts and Crafts colony, which championed individual craftsmanship in protest to the dehumanizing effects of the Industrial Revolution. Inspired, Hubbard came back and established an Arts and Crafts community in East Aurora, thereby founding the Arts and Crafts movement in America. The Roycroft Inn, one of the principal buildings on the campus, is a National Historic Landmark.

Tiffany window in Pullman Church, Albion.

• The great American architect Louis Sullivan is considered the father of the skyscraper. Sullivan's singular contribution to the skyscraper capital of the world, New York City, is the Bayard-Condict Building at 65-69 Bleecker Street. It is one of the earliest high-rise structures in America and was built in 1897-1899. Sullivan's early masterful skyscraper became the inspiration for New York City to become the first and foremost vertical metropolis in the world.

1900s

• A unique architectural feature of the Albright-Knox Art Gallery in Buffalo is the eight marble classical caryatids that support the side porches of the handsome 1905 building. The marble female figures were carved by America's preeminent sculptor of the time, Augustus St. Gaudens (1848-1907). He was paid $60,000 for the sculptures—the largest commission he had ever received and the last one he completed before his death.

• The first great Art Deco building in America is the Barclay-Vesey Building (now Verizon Building) in New York City. It was built in 1926. The innovative architect was 34-year-old Ralph Walker of McKenzie, Voorhees & Gmelin Architects.

Caryatids at Albright-Knox Art Gallery.

• The first highway in the United States with divided lanes and limited access is the Meadowbrook Causeway, which was completed in 1929 to provide mass access to the world's largest ocean beachfront facility, Jones Beach, on six miles of ocean frontage in Long Island. It was one of the largest public construction achievements of the 20th century, created by Robert Moses, president of the New York State Council of Parks and the Long Island State Park Commission.

• The largest museum of glass in the world is the 117,400-square-foot Corning Museum of Glass in Corning. It was completed in 1997. The spectacular glass building was designed by the architectural firm of Smith, Miller & Hawkinson, and the amazing and sensational exhibits were created by Ralph Appelbaum Associates.

Richard O. Reisem
August 2006

Jones Beach with watertower.

11

OLD WESTBURY: WESTBURY HOUSE

When John Shaffer ("Jay") Phipps (1874-1958), financier and sportsman, married Margarita C. ("Dita") Grace (1876-1957) in England in 1903, he asked her to move to America where Jay's father, Henry Phipps, was a partner with Andrew Carnegie and the largest stockholder in Carnegie Steel Company (later U.S. Steel). Dita—daughter of Michael Grace, who with his brother William founded Grace Steamship Company—was so reluctant to leave her beloved England that Jay promised her a handsome English country house with fine English furnishings and a proper English garden. Phipps bought 200 acres in Old Westbury and hired the London designer George Abraham Crawley, assisted by American architect Grosvenor Atterbury, to design the house, which was completed in 1906. It is a magnificent Charles II-style country house evocative of stately 18th-century Georgian architecture—a three-story mansion of red brick and limestone with an unusual cluster of chimneys spanned by open decorative arches and situated in the center of the roof. Seventy of the estate's 200 acres are elaborately landscaped into a series of splendid English gardens. There are grand early-18th-century wrought-iron gates created by Robert Bakewell and imported from England, making them arguably the finest English iron gates in America. The lavishly carved and sculpted interior, today a house museum, retains the entire Phipps collection of English antique furniture, artifacts, sculpture, and paintings, including such master painters as Sir Joshua Reynolds, Thomas Gainsborough, Sir Henry Raeburn, John Singer Sargent, and John Constable. The house is so authentic and splendid that it is often a setting for Hollywood motion pictures, including *The Age of Innocence*.

Left: The garden façade of Westbury House balances stone sculptures with sculpted shrubbery.

Top: A stone sphinx decorates the Westbury garden. In Greek mythology, the sphinx had a woman's head and a lion's body.

Overleaf: The Red Ballroom of Westbury House is lighted by crystal chandeliers at its four corners. The stone fireplace mantel features a marble maiden in the frieze.

Above: The wood-paneled dining room displays Old Master English portraits and a fireplace mantel supported by white marble caryatids.

Left: Overlooking the lake is a gazebo, the Temple of Love, with a dome of filigreed iron.

Right: The welcoming Front Hall features an elaborately carved stone chimneypiece.

OYSTER BAY: SAGAMORE HILL, THEODORE ROOSEVELT HOUSE

When Theodore Roosevelt was 25 years old, he married Alice Hathaway Lee, and the couple purchased land on a hill in Cove Neck with plans to build a summer house. But before construction began, Alice Lee Roosevelt died in 1884 two days after their child, also named Alice, was born. Roosevelt, however, determined to build the house to provide a suitable home for his young daughter. Completed in 1885, the house was called Sagamore Hill after the Indian chief, Sagamore Mohannis, who had previously signed away his rights to the land. Roosevelt remarried in 1886, this time to a childhood friend, Edith Kermit Carow. They moved into Sagamore Hill the following spring, and the Roosevelt family lived here for the rest of their lives, except for the times when Roosevelt's public career required his residence elsewhere. Above the front door is the family motto: "Qui Plantavit Curabit" (He Who Plants, Preserves), which refers to Sagamore Hill being a working farm. The house is a typical Victorian rambling structure, which was designed by the New York City architectural firm of Lamb and Rich and is of brick and wood-frame construction. Its three stories contain 23 rooms. Principal rooms on the first floor include the front hall, library, drawing room, dining room, pantry, kitchen, and the North Room, which is a spacious room added in 1905 to accommodate large gatherings at Sagamore Hill, which occurred frequently after Roosevelt became U.S. president in September 1901. The second floor contains bedrooms, nursery, guest rooms, and bathrooms. The Gun Room where Roosevelt often entertained friends is on the third floor as are servants' quarters for a staff of six, sewing room, and Theodore Roosevelt, Jr.'s bedroom. But the special quality of this house is the incredible collection of furnishings that were loved and used by the Roosevelt family.

Above: A windmill pumped well water on Teddy Roosevelt's working farm.

Right: The expansive front porch on President Theodore Roosevelt's summer White House overlooked the rolling landscape that stretched to Cold Spring Harbor.

Above: When the Roosevelts lived here, they could see the waters of Oyster Bay from the wraparound porch.

Right: The North Room at Sagamore Hill was added in 1905, allowing Roosevelt to entertain large groups.

Middle: The Gun Room on the top floor was Roosevelt's second office. It provided a quiet place to write.

Far Right: This small room off the master bedroom was Roosevelt's dressing room.

SAG HARBOR: BENJAMIN HUNTTING HOUSE

*T*wo hundred years ago, Sag Harbor and New York City were the two official New York State ports of entry. Sag Harbor was a thriving port with trading ships arriving and leaving for faraway lands around the globe. It was also a principal port for the whaling industry with a whaling wharf dating back to 1741. Sag Harbor's prosperity brought a wealth of landmark buildings including the 1693 House and every popular architectural style of the 19th century. A particular jewel, the Benjamin Huntting II House, is a striking Greek Revival mansion, Long Island's finest example of this architectural style. It was designed by Minard Lafever, the dominant Greek Revival architectural author and architect of the 19th century. Built in 1845, the house has a temple-fronted portico, ornate Corinthian columns, and interesting cresting above the cornice that proclaims Huntting's trade—alternating shapes of flensing knives and blubber spades around the entire roof line. Inside, there is a dramatic spiral staircase, exquisitely detailed plaster ceilings, carved door and window frames. It houses the Sag Harbor Whaling Museum today with a fascinating collection of harpoons, scrimshaw, model ships, and fine period furnishings. Benjamin Huntting II (1796-1867), like his father Col. Benjamin Huntting (1753-1807), was the owner of whaling ships and ship captain who made a fortune from whale oil, an important commodity in the 18th and 19th centuries. In 1845, he paid $7,000 to build this notable mansion that is considered a national treasure today.

Above: A graceful spiral staircase winds upward from the front hall of the Huntting House.

Right: The Benjamin Huntting House is a Greek Revival masterpiece designed by Minard Lafever. On the left, a small whaling boat is protected by a Greek Revival canopy.

SAG HARBOR: OLD CUSTOMS HOUSE

*I*n the early years of the 1800s, the two major ports in New York State were Sag Harbor and New York City. One of the very first bills passed in the first session of the U.S. Congress established New York City and Sag Harbor as the two official U.S. ports of entry in New York State. Henry P. Dering was named Sag Harbor's customs master in 1789, and he conducted federal business from his home, hence the residential appearance of the Old Customs House. One of Dering's sons took over as customs master after his father, so the Derings operated the customs business from this house for 60 years, until 1849. The Federal style frame house has 12-over-12 double-hung windows, all symmetrically placed on front and side façades.

SAG HARBOR: OLD WHALERS CHURCH

*I*n the 1800s, Sag Harbor was Long Island's whaling capital. More than 60 whaling ships with more than 800 men working on them sailed from Sag Harbor. In 1843, at the peak of the whaling period, the prominent New York City architect, Minard Lafever (1797-1854), was commissioned to design a church for this bustling whaling community. Although the most popular style of architecture at the time was Greek Revival and Lafever was one of its principal proponents, he published a series of pattern books on architecture of various styles and designed many buildings in a

number of styles besides Greek Revival, including neo-Gothic, Tudor Gothic, Collegiate Gothic, Romanesque, Italianate, and, rarely, Egyptian Revival. His notebooks, however, contained many sketches of Egyptian structures, monuments, and artifacts. The Sag Harbor church offered a perfect opportunity to design an Egyptian Revival style building, because the ancient Egyptians were, like Sag Harbor residents, considered a seafaring people. The façade, composed of three massive vertical elements, is reminiscent of ancient Egyptian temple pylons. The walls flare out at the base as they do in Egyptian architecture, and the windows are tall and slit-like. Then, to make the church even more specific to Sag Harbor's whaling industry, Lafever incorporated decorative motifs that reflected the whaling trade, such as the wood cresting above the cornice in the shape of flensing paddles used to cut whale blubber. The result, completed in 1844, is one of the most significant large Egyptian style structures in America. Originally, the church had a 187-foot, telescoping steeple—the tallest wooden example of its kind in the world. The steeple contained four clocks made by the famous Sherry & Byram Clock Works in Sag Harbor. Ephraim Byram's large clocks were manufactured for steeples and street posts all along the U.S. east coast in the 19th century. The tower, however, did not survive. It was destroyed in the fierce hurricane of September 1938.

Above: The Old Customs House in Sag Harbor was a residence built in the 1700s.

Right: The unusual Egyptian style Old Whalers Church stands behind a whalers' burial ground.

OYSTER BAY: COE HALL

*I*n the early decades of the 20th century, when the Long Island Railroad permitted easy access to the island, the north shore of Nassau County became prime real estate for summer houses of wealthy New Yorkers. The area from Roslyn to Huntington, with its many lavish estates, became known as the Gold Coast. In the middle of this posh strip is the historic village of Oyster Bay and just a couple of miles from town on Chicken Valley Road is the 409-acre estate of William Robertson Coe—an Englishman who made a fortune investing in real estate, railroads, mining, and insurance—and his wife, Mai Huttleston Rogers, heiress of a Standard Oil Company fortune. Between 1913 and the 1930s, they built an incredible estate known today as Planting Fields Arboretum State Historic Park. Magnificent stone and iron gates—made in Surrey, England in 1711—greet visitors at the main entrance. Several landscape architects, including the Olmsted Brothers, created 200 acres of lush gardens with exotic specimen trees from all over the world and 20 specialty gardens. Coe Hall is a massive 65-room English Tudor Revival manor house constructed between 1918 and 1921. It was designed by the architectural firm of Walker and Gillette and built of Indiana limestone. The renowned London interior designer Charles Duveen decorated the house with fine art and antiques. There are rooms of expansive grandeur as well as of cozy scale for every imaginable activity and purpose, including a telephone room, an octagonal sitting room, and a breakfast room covered with a mural of buffaloes. Each of the 11 bedrooms has its own bath. Here, the Coe family led a glamorous life of yachting, polo, and social engagements. William Coe died in 1955.

Left: Twisted limestone columns flank the elaborate Coe Hall front entrance with its shallow-arched double doors.

Above: An enclosed porch forms the entrance projection on the façade of Coe Hall.

Below: One of the many charming buildings on the Coe family estate is this picturesque cottage with a great sloping roof that ends in an eyebrow eave over the front entrance.

Left: Wood beams form a shallow-arched ceiling in the expansive gallery with stone arches and floor at Coe Hall.

Above: A cozy sitting room is octagonal in shape and is lighted by a massive glass chandelier.

Right: English Tudor details include triple Roman arches with a Sun God carved in stone above.

ISLIP: W. BAYARD CUTTING ESTATE

William Bayard Cutting (1850-1912) was an entrepreneur who became wealthy building railroads, operating the ferries of New York City, and developing the south Brooklyn waterfront. In 1888, he started a sugar-beet industry in the U.S. He was also a sportsman, a lover of nature, and a superb gardener. In 1880, he purchased an estate on the south shore of Long Island from Pierre Lorillard and began creating a 690-acre arboretum by importing trees and shrubs, particularly conifers, from all over the world to add to the existing aggregation. He hired the great Frederick Law Olmsted to landscape the grounds. For his mansion, he commissioned New York City architect Charles C. Haight (1841-1917) to design it. Haight was best known for his designs of institutional buildings including several at Columbia University. The massive, rambling, three-story house was built between 1886-1890 and combines Shingle and Tudor styles with multiple half-timbered gables, tall enormous chimneys, a sweeping piazza, eyebrow windows, and a three-story tower. Inside there are magnificent stone fireplaces, fine hand-carved woodwork, and two splendid Tiffany stained-glass windows in the stair hall. There is even a museum of stuffed birds. From the piazza a great lawn slopes down to the Connetquot River. The welcoming house and incredible grounds make the estate a particularly fine place to visit, roam, and relax.

Below: A tree-lined walk along the Connetquot River.

Right: Fine hand-carved woodwork adorns the parlor of the Cutting House.

*Left: Purple-and-white cleomes bloom
along a walk in the garden.*

*Top: The spacious master bedroom of
the William Bayard Cutting House.*

*Above: A classic bench faces gardens
designed by Frederick Law Olmsted.*

*Right: The Tudor influence is seen in
the ceiling and massive chimneypiece
of a sitting room.*

GRAND CENTRAL TERMINAL

*C*ommuter trains destined for America's greatest city are aimed at Grand Central Terminal, built 1903-1913 in the heart of Manhattan. As they near their destination, the trains dive into a two-and-a-half-mile tunnel that burrows beneath the glitter and swank of Park Avenue. From 50th Street south, the railroad tracks fan out onto two underground levels that stretch from Madison Avenue to the west and Lexington Avenue to the east. Above all this, skyscrapers hide the presence of the vast railroad yard beneath them. This ingenious design that permits two levels of arrivals and is invisible from Manhattan streets was the work of the architectural engineering firm, Reed & Stem, with William J. Wilgus, chief of construction for New York Central Railroad, being the brilliant railroad engineer who worked out the clever plan using ramps instead of stairs and spreading 70 underground railroad tracks far beyond the terminal building's footprint. Above ground, Grand Central Terminal is equally impressive. The terminal building was designed by Warren & Wetmore with the principal architect being Whitney Warren. It is a Beaux-Arts extravaganza with three huge Roman arches on the façade, as if announcing a grand entrance to an ancient walled city. A series of double columns frame the archways. Above the central arch is an elaborately embellished clock that is surrounded by sculptures of three classical figures. The sculptural group was created by Jules-Alexis Coutane and includes Mercury on top, representing speed, Hercules on the left and Minerva on the right, symbolizing strength and contemplation, all attributes claimed by New York Central Railroad, builders of Grand Central. The barrel-vaulted ceiling in the grand concourse (275 feet long, 120 feet wide, and 125 feet high) is a mural depicting the night sky with its constellations. The electrified stars twinkle 24 hours a day.

Three classical figures surround the clock above the entrance to Grand Central Station.

BROOKLYN BRIDGE

*T*he Brooklyn Bridge was the first great suspension bridge in the world. When it opened in 1883, after 13 years of construction, it was hailed as an engineering marvel. The great man behind the great bridge was John Augustus Roebling (1806-1869), who was born in Prussia, studied engineering in Berlin, and emigrated to the United States at the age of 25 years. In 1841, Roebling established a factory in Saxonburg, Pennsylvania, to manufacture wire rope. He developed a theory that bridges could be suspended from his wire ropes and tested the idea by constructing several small suspension bridges before undertaking the massive Brooklyn Bridge spanning the East River to connect two islands, Manhattan and Long Island, the location of Brooklyn. Roebling died just before construction started, and his son, Washington Roebling, managed the project to completion, even though he was stricken by caisson disease

(the bends) and had to direct activities from his bed. The bends was an illness of workers who labored constructing foundations in the deep underwater caissons where the water was kept out by air pressure. The bends resulted from too rapid decompression when coming out of compressed air. No accident records were kept, but it is estimated that between 20 and 50 workers died from the bends, cable failure, an explosion, and a fire that burned for weeks. Others died when crushed by falling stone, caught in machinery, and falling into the water. But the result was spectacular. Sixteen-inch-thick steel cables swoop down from two massive stone neo-Gothic towers from which a lacework of steel cables creates a spiderweb effect. The whole bridge is 6,016 feet long, and the central span is 1,596 feet, the longest in the world for many years. The bridge cost $17,909,000 in 1880s dollars.

FEDERAL HALL NATIONAL MEMORIAL

*I*n the early years of our nation, the culture of ancient Greece with its democratic institutions and grand architecture captured the admiration of Americans. Greek architecture—specifically the Parthenon with its elegance, symmetry, and stateliness—became the inspiration for architects Town & Davis (Alexander Jackson Davis and Ithiel Town) in designing the U.S. Custom House at Wall and Broad streets. The imposing marble building in masculine Greek Doric style is now the Federal Hall National Memorial. The massive structure was begun in 1834 and completed in 1842. By 1844, the young Boston architect Arthur D. Gilman became the building's most vituperative critic, condemning it as an "incongruous and absurd pile." He said, "Everyone is weary of the eternal Grecian with its ostentatious meanness and stilted pretension." Although Gilman became a prominent architect, designing primarily in the French Second Empire style, Federal Hall remains much-loved as a museum today, and its rotunda is among the finest Greek Revival spaces in New York City with its saucer dome, Corinthian columns, and iron railings formed of twisting vines and classical female sculptures. It was on this site in 1789 in the original Federal Hall where George Washington took the oath of office as the first president of the new republic.

WASHINGTON ARCH

*I*n 1889, New York City celebrated the centennial of George Washington's inauguration as the first president of the United States—an event that had occurred in New York City itself in 1789. A wealthy lawyer, William Rhinelander Stewart, proposed a temporary arch be erected at the foot of Fifth Avenue and suggested that 35-year-old Stanford White design it. White was a partner in the great New York City architectural firm, McKim, Mead & White that formed in 1879. The wood-and-plaster arch was so successful that a cry went up for a permanent marble version. Again, White was the architect. He wrote, "In style, this monument is distinctly classic, and by this term is meant Roman, ... which seems proper in the design of a structure intended to stand for all time and to outlast any local or passing fashions." The sculptures and bas relief decoration were created by Frederick MacMonnies. Enormous praise descended on White for his masterful design, but at the dedication on May 4, 1895, of the 70-foot marble arch, one of the speakers, General Horace Porter, glared at White and announced that "the true purpose of this work is not the display of architectural skill, but the perpetuation of the memory of the exalted patriot who founded this republic." He then went on to describe Washington, as some observers noted, in terms that remarkably resembled General Porter himself. But as one journalist wrote, "We began to think there was such a thing as beauty in architecture, and the name of Stanford White was on every tongue."

BROOKLYN BOTANIC GARDEN

*I*n the Brooklyn of the 1800s, ashes produced by burning coal to run manufactories and heat homes and commercial establishments were hauled to a site that is now 1000 Washington Avenue and dumped there. From this beginning as an ash dump and with a hope that the massive accumulation of inorganic material on the site would not hurt, and perhaps enhance, the growth of organic materials, New York State reserved 30 acres of the dump for a botanic garden in 1897. With the hiring of Dr. Charles Stuart Gager as the first director, the garden opened in 1910. If anything, the ash enhanced organic growth, because today more than 10,000 kinds of plants populate the hugely verdant Brooklyn Botanic Garden that has grown to 52 acres of immaculate lawns and gardens, an esplanade of cherry trees, and some outstanding architecture. There is a $25-million Steinhardt Conservatory built in 1988 that now houses the world's oldest and largest bonsai (dwarf-tree) collection. A Beaux-Arts style structure, called the Palm House, hosts special events for 300 guests. The spectacular centerpiece of the Brooklyn Botanic Garden is the Japanese Hill-and-Pond Garden, created in 1915 by the famous Japanese landscape designer, Takeo Shiota (1881-1943). Among its architectural structures are a Shinto temple and wooden bridges. Stone antique lanterns decorate the winding hilly paths that lead to a waterfall and a pond filled with carp and turtles, and featuring an island in this stunning setting. The Japanese Garden underwent extensive renovation in 1999 and was rededicated in 2000.

Above: The Japanese Hill-and-Pond Garden was created in 1915.

Left: A neoclassical octagonal tower greets visitors entering the Brooklyn Botanic Garden.

Right: The Rose Garden is one of several spectacular features in the 52 acres of the garden.

CHRYSLER BUILDING

America's favorite Art Deco skyscraper is clearly the Chrysler Building, 405 Lexington Avenue at 42nd Street. And for one year, 1930, it was the tallest building in the world. It was designed by an architect, William Van Alen (1882-1954), who rejected classical traditions and opted for a more futuristic style and novel building materials. He had the good fortune to team up with Walter P. Chrysler (1875-1940), a nouveau-riche industrialist, who wanted to make a dramatic statement for his hugely successful automobile manufactory with a new company office building in midtown Manhattan. Van Alen planned a sleek, inventive building for Chrysler that would be the tallest in the world, but then a competitive architect, H. Craig Severance, eager to trump his former partner Van Alen and be the architect of the tallest building, designed the Bank of Manhattan 30 feet higher. Van Alen and Chrysler secretly plotted at the last minute to extend the height of the Chrysler Building by adding a spire, a cloud-piercing needle that was the most complex geometric structure imagined anywhere in 1929. It was an extravagant fantasy made of diamond-honed Enduro KA-2 steel (stainless chromium-nickel steel), a new product developed by Krupp in Germany, whose silver glow no amount of exposure would ever tarnish. (Not a single sheet of it has ever been replaced in the Chrysler Building in its 76 years.) The spire was secretly assembled inside the almost-finished structure and hoisted into place to make the Chrysler Building 1,046 feet and 4 3/4 inches high, the tallest in the world. One year later, in 1931, the 1,250-foot Empire State Building was built.

FLATIRON BUILDING

At 23rd Street in Manhattan, Broadway crosses Fifth Avenue at an extremely narrow angle, creating a lot that comes to a sharp point. Most architects viewed the triangular site as incapable of containing a tall building. The George F. Fuller Company, however, thought differently and hired the great Chicago architect, Daniel H. Burnham, to design a 286-foot, 21-story skyscraper for the site. At the Broadway-Fifth Avenue intersection, the building would be so narrow, a mere six feet wide, that people feared it would topple over in the wind, which was particularly gusty at that intersection. But because Burnham's bold design included heavy diagonal steel wind-bracing at the corner of each bay, the building has not toppled, and the gusty wind remains. Built between 1901 and 1903, the skyscraper was first called the Fuller Building, but the structure's narrow prow caught the imagination of New Yorkers, who gave it a permanent name, Flatiron Building. It is one of the first skyscrapers, which are buildings entirely supported on a steel skeleton frame. The stonework and terra cotta, with which it is covered, are just a skin to keep out that gusty weather. Burnham made the building look indestructible by covering it with bold neo-French Renaissance details in stone and terra cotta. In 1907, painter John Sloane noticed that the gusts around the Flatiron Building caused women's skirts to flap over their heads, and he painted the scene. It became a famous postcard, which attracted men to the site to see the action live, which, in turn, caused the policeman on that corner to shoo away oglers with the cry, "Hey, you on 23, skidoo."

BROOKLYN: GREEN-WOOD CEMETERY

*T*he spectacular entrance gates to Green-Wood Cemetery at Fifth Avenue and 25th Street in Brooklyn promise high drama within. Two soaring gables with pierced tracery and other Gothic details like turrets, crockets, and spires indicate the highly dramatic architectural style of Victorian Gothic Revival. It was achieved, in this case, by America's greatest architect of the Gothic style, Richard Upjohn, who, with help from his architect son, designed and supervised the erection of these gates and contiguous buildings with multicolored slate roofs, all accomplished during the Civil War, from 1861 to 1865. The gates amply announce one of America's first and most prestigious cemeteries opened in 1840 and now filling 478 acres with 560,000 permanent residents. Among the hills, ponds, winding roads, and thickly wooded landscape, there are superb views over New York City harbor and lower Manhattan and a multitude of funerary art, sculpture, and mausoleums. Interred among the picturesque monuments are such famous people as Henry Ward Beecher (abolitionist), James Gordon Bennett (started *New York Herald*), Leonard Bernstein (composer and conductor), DeWitt Clinton (NY governor, Erie Canal), Peter Cooper (builder of first locomotive, laid Atlantic Cable), Nathaniel Currier & James M. Ives (artists), T. C. Durant (head of Union Pacific Railroad), Charles H. Ebbets (president of Brooklyn Dodgers), Horace Greeley (newspaper editor), Elias Howe (inventor of sewing machine), Samuel F. B. Morse (inventor of telegraph), James Renwick, Jr., (architect of St. Patrick's Cathedral and Smithsonian Institution), Henry E. Steinway (piano maker), Charles Lewis Tiffany (founder of Tiffany & Company), William Marcy (Boss) Tweed (Tammany Hall), 38 Union and 2 Confederate generals, and more than a half-a-million more.

SURROGATE'S COURT

*T*he Beaux-Arts style, with its exuberant ornamentation, is well represented by the Surrogate's Court building at the corner of Chambers and Centre streets. The tall mansard roof section on top of the cornice is depicted above. Here are elaborately framed dormer windows arranged symmetrically, which is an important characteristic of the Beaux-Arts style. Also typical of the style are decorative garlands, floral patterns, and shields. The seven-story building, with a row of classical Corinthian columns across the façade, was designed to be fireproof, since it was originally intended to house city records, so it is of steel-frame construction clad in Maine granite. Surrogate's Court is an example of the early 20th-century "City Beautiful" movement. The purpose of this movement was to provide cities with awe-inspiring classical buildings to create an ennobling experience for citizens. Part of that experience depended on sculpture, so two great sculptors, Philip Martiny and Henry K. Bush-Brown, created 54 classical statues to adorn the exterior of the building. They are mostly of historic New York figures like DeWitt Clinton and Peter Stuyvesant. With all of its grand features and embellishments, the building took eight years to complete, from 1899 to 1907. The distinguished architect of Surrogate's Court was John Rochester Thomas from Rochester, New York. He never saw his completed masterpiece, because he died in the Thousand Islands in the summer of 1901 at age 53 years.

ELLIS ISLAND NATIONAL MONUMENT

*E*llis Island sits in New York harbor not far from the Statue of Liberty. Before the Revolutionary War, it was a hangout for pirates; the U.S. bought it from New York in 1808 and built a fort there to defend the harbor from the British in the War of 1812. Then, on January 1, 1892, the first U.S. immigration station, built of Georgia pine, opened for business, only to burn to the ground in 1897. The U.S. government decreed that all future buildings on Ellis Island had to be fireproof. And the architectural firm of Boring and Tilton was engaged to design that first fireproof building, the Main Hall, now the Ellis Island Immigration Museum. It opened on December 17, 1900 and received 2,251 immigrants on opening day.

Those immigrants faced an imposing building designed in French Renaissance Revival style. It is a grand brick and limestone structure with three triumphal arches at the entrance and impressive towers at the corners of the façade, certainly a majestic sight for the poor immigrants. Most of the immigrants arrived before 1924 and climbed the steep stairs to the great, echoing Registry Room, where they faced legal and medical inspections. Between 1892 and 1954, more than 12 million immigrants were processed through Ellis Island. A six-year renovation project costing $162 million was completed in 1990, and the Ellis Island Immigration Museum was opened to the public on September 10, 1990.

Right: Immigrants faced legal and medical inspections in the huge Registry Room with a high vaulted ceiling.

NEW YORK PUBLIC LIBRARY

*M*unicipally funded building projects rarely become masterpieces of architecture, but the New York Public Library—through the coercive efforts of its architects, Carrère & Hastings—became one of the finest examples of Beaux-Arts design in America. Early estimates placed the cost of the library at $2.5 million. It ended up costing $9,002,523.09. The city pushed for a façade of brick and terra cotta, with limestone as an acceptable alternative. But Carrère & Hastings pitched for white marble and won. The architects specified the purest marble from the quarry in Dorset, Vermont, but rejected 65 percent of the stone delivered. The massive library façade on Fifth Avenue stretched two blocks (350 feet) between 40th and 42nd streets and was constructed between 1898-1911. It consolidated the private book collections of the Astor Library, the Lenox Library, and the Tilden Trust. A projecting pavilion with three arches and broad front stairs lead the public into one of the world's foremost research institutions. Embellishing the exterior are a pair of lions sculpted by Edward Clark Potter, fountains by Frederick MacMonnies, classical figures above the entrances by Paul Wayland Bartlett, and the decorative end pediments by George Gray Barnard. The chief architect, John M. Carrère, was killed in an automobile accident just weeks before the library opened. He lay in state in the great hall in 1911, and his bust is permanently on display in a niche by the grand staircase.

Top: The great entrance hall of the library.

Above: The reading room of the public library.

MORRIS-JUMEL MANSION

American history was made in the 1765 Morris-Jumel Mansion, 65 Jumel Terrace. The builder of this imposing Georgian style house was Roger Morris, a colonel in the British army. The double-height portico with triangular pediment was a particularly innovative feature in 1765. Also, the interior has the country's first octagonal room. In 1776, he abandoned the house and its 140-acre estate just in time to escape the Battle of Harlem Heights, George Washington's first Revolutionary War victory. Washington commandeered the empty house as his headquarters. After the war in 1810, the house was purchased by Stephen Jumel, a wealthy French shipping magnate from Santo Domingo, who promptly died leaving the mansion to his socialite wife, Madame Eliza Jumel, who became New York's richest widow. She went on to have a stormy two-year marriage to Aaron Burr, whom she married when he was 78 years old. Madame Jumel entertained lavishly in the three-story house with a colonnaded portico and with French furniture that she claimed was given to her by Napoleon Bonaparte. She was a close friend of Lafayette, Talleyrand, Benjamin Franklin, and Patrick Henry. In 1904, the mansion was turned into a house museum. Washington's bedroom has been restored to 1776; the dining room reflects the decor when Washington returned to the house in 1790 for a famous lunch with John Adams, Alexander Hamilton, John Quincy Adams, and Thomas Jefferson. Other rooms evoke Madame Eliza Jumel's elegant French taste applied to fine Georgian architecture.

Above: The dining room where George Washington entertained is fitted with fine French Empire style furniture.

Left: In this parlor, General George Washington made battle plans during the Revolutionary War.

Right: Madame Eliza Jumel's bedroom contains furniture that she claimed was given to her by Napoleon.

GREENPORT: OLANA

*T*he matchless beauty of the Hudson River Valley inspired a school of painting in the 19th century that became known as the Hudson River School. The preeminent painter of the movement was Frederic Edwin Church (1826-1900), a master of 19th-century landscape painting. He became famous and wealthy for his paintings, including huge panoramic works like *Niagara* and *The Heart of the Andes,* for which thousands of people stood in line to pay the admission to see them. Church's second love was the house, Olana, he built for himself and his family high above the Hudson River with spectacular views of the river and the Catskill Mountains. Church and his wife Isabel took a trip to the Middle East in 1867 where they were enormously impressed with Islamic architecture and decoration. He wanted his new house in America to reflect "Persian architecture," as he called it. Church had acquired the hilltop in 1867, and after returning from the Middle East, he collaborated with the New York City architect, Calvert Vaux, partner of the great landscape architect Frederick Law Olmsted, to begin the design and construction of the main house, a Moorish fantasy, from 1870 to 1873. A studio wing, designed by Church on his own, was added between 1888 and 1891. In 1884, he wrote concerning his progress at Olana, "I have made about one and three-quarters miles of roads this season, opening entirely new and beautiful views. I can make more and better landscapes in this way than by tampering with canvas and paint in the studio." He also doted on the elaborate design of the house. It is a massive limestone structure with three towers, enclosing bells, water reservoir, and painting studio. There are Moorish arches, projecting balconies, bay windows, recessed porches, all covered with roofs of red, blue, and green slate. The house is covered with oriental ornament of colored brick and tile. Inside is a world of exotic, oriental magnificence.

KINGSTON: SENATE HOUSE

*T*he Senate House, built in 1676, was actually the private residence of the Van Gaasbeek family. Even though the Dutch colony of New Netherland surrendered to English forces on August 29, 1664 and became the English colony of New York, this house, built just 12 years later, is still very much designed and constructed in the Dutch style. It is made of solid Ulster County limestone. Roofs of Dutch houses were steeper than those of English houses because they suited the weather in the Netherlands where wind-blown rain could penetrate under tiles on lower-pitched roofs and cause them to leak. Of course, wooden shingles were often substituted in New Netherland, but the steep roof was still retained in the New World. Early Dutch houses had a small number of rooms, but those rooms were usually quite large, which gave this house a role in the first New York State government in 1777. So, at the beginning of the Revolutionary War, when the British captured and occupied New York City from 1776 to 1783, the fledgling New York State government fled the city and moved to Kingston in Ulster County, where the county courthouse served as the capitol and the site of the Supreme Court. The State Assembly met in a tavern, but at the invitation of the Van Gaasbeeks, the Senate, which at the time had 24 members, met in this house. Hence, its historic significance as the Senate House.

Top left: After the British captured New York City, the fledgling state senate met in this room.

Bottom left: Detail of inkwell beside the Windsor chair above.

Above: The front parlor of the Senate House has wide-plank floors, 12-over-12 double-hung windows, and a high mantel above the large fireplace.

Right: The Van Gaasbeek family built their limestone house in 1676.

NEW PALTZ: HUGUENOT STREET

*T*he village of New Paltz was founded in 1678 by 12 French families, who belonged to a Protestant sect, called Huguenots, who were persecuted by the Catholic King Louis XIV and fled from France for refuge in die Pfalz on the Rhine River in Germany. Learning of religious freedom in America, they emigrated to New York, bought 40,000 acres from the Esopus Indians in 1677, and named their community center New Paltz. The Catskill Mountains provided limestone and wood for building a unique street of houses and a church on Huguenot Street, the oldest street in America with its original houses, that looks much the same today as it did by 1792. The French church is a reconstruction of the original 1717 structure. The steeply pitched roof of the squarish stone church is topped by a cupola from which a horn or giant conch shell was blown to call members to a service. Of the six stone houses on the street, the Jean Hasbrouck House and the Abraham Hasbrouck House (they were brothers who, incidentally,

married sisters) were both built in 1694 and display particularly interesting architectural features. The Jean Hasbrouck House has chimneys on two interior partition walls, thereby permitting fireplaces in rooms on both sides of the wall. The chimneys are staggering in size, being 3 by 9 feet at the base and 26 feet high to the roof line. The high-pitched, Dutch-style roof is so enormous that to ensure its strength against strong winds and snow load, the roof structure had to include extra bracing. One of the dramatic features of the Abraham Hasbrouck House is its exposed chimney, which provides a flue for a cooking fireplace in the cellar. With its wide base curving gracefully to a narrower chimney, this well built brick smokestack has served well for 300 years. The Bevier-Elting House, built in 1698, includes a verandah on the long side. Also, the top section of the end gables, like the Jean Hasbrouck House, are unusual, being constructed of wood rather than continuing the limestone.

Above: One of the six residences on Huguenot Street has a shed roof over the entrance.

Top: To lighten the load on the stone walls, the upper portion of the gables were constructed of wood.

Above: Symmetrical placement of fenestrations on all exterior wall surfaces was important, as can be seen in the Jean Hasbrouck House.

Right: The steep-roofed, square French church is a reconstruction of the 1717 original.

GARRISON: BOSCOBEL

*T*he design of one of the most outstanding Federal style houses in America cannot be attributed to any known American architect, yet the refinement of its every element shows consummate taste and intimate knowledge of the style, which in New York State was popular between 1780 and 1820. The mystery may be solved by considering its owner, States Morris Dyckman (1755-1806), a descendant of early Dutch settlers in New Amsterdam. States Dyckman, although born in America, worked in England from 1778 to 1789 and became a close friend of William Adam, a nephew of the great architect, Robert Adam, who created the great English houses of the 18th century and which became the inspiration for Federal style architecture in America. Dyckman's superlative taste and close familiarity with the works of Robert Adam points to him as the likely creator of Boscobel. Or perhaps he brought back from England an Adamesque house design. When he returned to America in 1789, Dyckman brought with him an exceptional collection of English candelabra, china, silver, crystal, and books, now displayed at Boscobel. The front elevation of the wood-frame house is particularly distinguished. A rarely seen feature is the carved wooden swags of drapery with bowknots and tassels that hang from the pediment between the slender columns of the second-floor balcony. The tripartite windows with large glass panes and slender muntins were uncommon in America when this house was built between 1804 and 1808. They give the house a sophisticated appearance and provide brightly lighted interior spaces. A household inventory of 1806 was discovered in the Dyckman papers and made possible a truly historic restoration of the interior, which among many fine pieces, contains an unrivaled collection of Duncan Phyfe Federal furniture and cabinetry. Boscobel was rescued from imminent demolition in 1955, disassembled, and stored for rebuilding on a new site 15 miles north of its original location. The reconstructed Boscobel opened in 1961.

Top: The double parlors are distinguished for their fine collection of New York Federal furniture.

Above: A bronze-urn fountain sends up a spire of water in the lily pond with the Hudson River and West Point beyond the trees.

Top: A magnificent drum-shaped writing table, attributed to Duncan Phyfe, dominates the library on the second floor of Boscobel.

Above: A second-floor bedroom is comprised of Federal style furniture and fabrics.

Right: The grand staircase, with its superb neoclassical details and distinctive wallpaper and carpeting, is a masterpiece of early 19th-century American architecture.

ANNANDALE-ON-HUDSON: MONTGOMERY PLACE

Montgomery Place, looking at its exterior, could be called a trompe l'oeil house, with its "fool the eye" façade. The walls seem to be constructed of fine cut stone. And the elegant fluted classical columns with Corinthian capitals, could they be carved of Italian white marble? Actually, the exterior walls of Montgomery Place are fieldstone covered with stucco that has been painted (with sand added to the paint) and scored to imitate cut stone. And the rest of the house—with its Classical Revival porches, porticos, terraces, columns, balustrades, cornices, and urns on pedestals—is carved wood. This elaborately detailed exterior is the sensitive, clever work of the most notable American architect of the 19th century, Alexander Jackson Davis (1803-1892). Davis did not design this house from scratch. Janet Livingston Montgomery, the widow of General Richard Montgomery who was killed in the Battle of Quebec in 1775, built the original structure in 1804-1805 as a dignified fieldstone farmhouse which Davis, in 1841 and again in 1863, transformed into an imposing refined Classical Revival mansion. He added three porches, a long verandah, and a wing on the south side. The inviting pentagonal north porch, with an awesome view of the Hudson River and the Catskill Mountains, is regarded as one of the first outdoor living rooms in America. The outstanding grounds were designed by the great landscape architect of the period, Andrew Jackson Downing (1815-1852).

Above: Elegant Montgomery Place looks like fine marble, but it is stucco over fieldstone and carved wood.

Far left: The north porch offers splendid views of the Hudson River and mountains beyond.

Left: Landscape architect Andrew Jackson Downing designed the grounds.

SLEEPY HOLLOW: PHILIPSBURG MANOR

Vredryck Flypsen (1626-1702) emigrated from Holland to New Netherland in America at the age of 21 years. By 1664 when the Dutch colony became British, he was already a very wealthy man. He quickly Anglicized his name to Frederick Philipse and continued his career as entrepreneur, merchant, landowner, ship owner, and slave trader that made him one of the richest men in the colony. He acquired a 52,000-acre estate, which covered much of what is Westchester County today. Philipsburg Manor was a commercial outpost for the international trading company operated by Frederick and his wealthy wife Margaret and which was head-quartered in New York City. The house at Sleepy Hollow, not being the Philipse primary residence, is a modest building of white-washed fieldstone built in 1680 and containing offices as well as living quarters. Its eight rooms, nevertheless, are elegant with William and Mary period furniture, 18th-century painted cupboards from the Netherlands, the earliest Chinese export porcelain to be found in the colony, world maps from the 1700s, and historic books and writing instruments. The collection of 17th- and 18th-century Dutch, English, and colonial American furnishings is one of the finest in America. The estate included a 1680s church where Philipse is buried (also Washington Irving), warehouse, Dutch three-aisle commercial dairy barn, wharf, slave house, bake house, and a great flour mill that ground wheat from tenant farmers on the 52,000 acres. The mill, still operating today, produced flour that was marketed in the northeast and Europe. On surrounding farms, there were fields of corn, wheat, barley, oats, rye, squash, pump-kins, beans, and peas. Peas were a big commercial crop shipped to markets in New York City and beyond.

Above: Not being the Philipse primary residence, the manor house is modest, constructed of whitewashed fieldstone. In the foreground, a well provides water.

Left: The flour mill, powered by a water-wheel, is at left, next to the residence/office, with a barn to the right.

Below: The Dutch, English, and colonial American furnishings in Philipsburg Manor are one of the finest in the country.

TARRYTOWN: KYKUIT, ROCKEFELLER ESTATE

*K*ykuit (rhymes with high cut) is the Dutch word for "Lookout," and that is very much the situation for this refined 40-room mansion and estate with a panoramic view of the Hudson River and the Palisades beyond. Kykuit has been the home of three Rockefellers—John D., Sr. (1839-1937), John D., Jr., and Nelson A.—from 1908 until 1979. Each put their personal stamp on the property. The original eclectic-style house of John D. Rockefeller, Sr. was unusually modest, but the famously frugal Standard Oil magnate maintained that he didn't want a palatial house, but rather, a comfortable one. The first version of Kykuit was completed in 1908 from plans initially drawn by Dunham A. Wheeler and revised by Chester Aldrich of Delano & Aldrich, with interiors by Ogden Codman. This version did not please either the Rockefellers or the multiple designers. The gardens by William Welles Bosworth,

however, were excellent—more elaborate and complex than the house. But the fireplaces smoked; kitchen deliveries below JDR's bedroom disturbed his sleep; guest rooms were too small, and on and on. Major reconstruction, more or less under John D., Jr.'s supervision, occurred from 1911 to 1913. Now, Bosworth designed an imposing classical façade to complement his Italianate gardens, and other changes made the house much grander than John D., Sr. had envisioned. Nevertheless, when he moved back in at the age of 74 years, he enjoyed his new house until he died at age 98 in 1937. John D., Jr., who loved beautiful things and fine design, lived in the house until his death in 1960, when his son, Nelson A., moved in and made the house a stunning museum for his spectacular collection of art and sculpture.

Above: Nelson Rockefeller added 20th-century bronze sculptures to the Inner Garden.

Left: William Welles Bosworth (1869-1966), who designed the gardens at Kykuit, created one of the finest and largest Beaux-Arts gardens in America.

Left: The music room, now missing its Aeolian pipe organ, has an oculus in the ceiling with a balustrade and dome above. The wall where organ pipes once stood now displays the painting, Hirondelle Amour by Joan Miro.

Top: The drawing room was designed by the much-admired interior designer, Ogden Codman, Jr. (1862-1951).

Above left: The Temple of Venus, a major architectural feature in the garden, houses a sculpture of Venus.

Above right: Looking through an archway into the library of Kykuit.

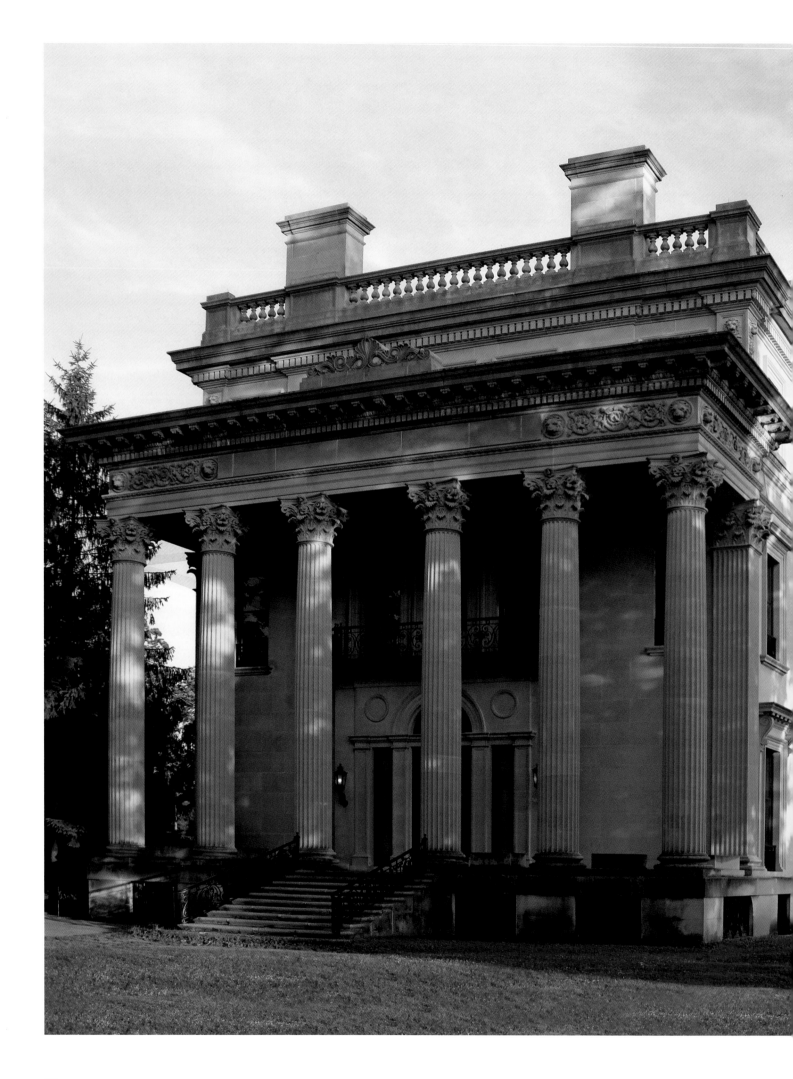

HYDE PARK: FREDERICK VANDERBILT MANSION

*T*he Vanderbilts liked palatial quarters and the Frederick Vanderbilt Mansion is consistent with the trend. It may not be the grandest of the many Vanderbilt houses, but it is one of the finest. And the reason for that is that it was designed by the greatest architects of the time: McKim, Mead & White. Charles F. McKim (1847-1909) was the principal architect, designing the exterior and basic interior structure. He selected a stately Beaux Arts style, a square form clad in Indiana limestone, and the classical Corinthian order, reminiscent of the imposing Renaissance palazzos of the Medici. There are many other elements of European origin in the house. In fact, Stanford White, McKim's partner, traveled to Europe and found many antique as well as new furnishings for the house, including a 17th-century coffered ceiling with painted murals, massive antique stone fireplace mantels, old tapestries, furniture, carpets, French silk velvet for draperies, and more. White, who was a genius at interior design, created the formal dining room in Renaissance style. The table and chairs he selected serve 18 guests. Ogden Codman, a designer who collaborated with Edith Wharton, created Mrs. Vanderbilt's exquisite bedroom, and Georges A. Glaenzer, a French decorator, designed Mr. Vanderbilt's princely suite as well as the den/library. The house, completed in 1898, has 54 rooms and required a staff of 20 servants, plus 40 more to maintain the lavish grounds. Frederick William Vanderbilt (1856-1938) was the grandson of Cornelius Vanderbilt. When his father, William Henry Vanderbilt, died, Frederick inherited $10 million, which he managed to increase to $80 million by the time of his death. He married Louise Holmes Anthony in 1878, and although the couple had residences in New York City, Newport, Bar Harbor, Palm Beach, and the Adirondacks, they were particularly fond of Hyde Park. And for good reason, as any visitor to the house today can testify.

Opposite page: The baronial dining room was designed by Stanford White in Renaissance style.

Left: The living room walls are paneled in Circassian walnut with elaborately carved walnut panels over two matching Italian marble fireplaces.

Above: The formal Italian gardens contrast with naturalistic landscaping on the rest of the estate.

Below: Louise Vanderbilt's bedroom is designed in Louis XV style with a curved railing separating the bed from the room.

TARRYTOWN: LYNDHURST

*L*yndhurst is America's greatest Gothic Revival castle. This masterpiece of picturesque architecture is the creation of Alexander Jackson Davis (1803-1892), the preeminent American architect of the Gothic style in the 19th century. The Hudson River Valley is the perfect setting for this romantic castle with castellated turrets, great stone chimneys, expansive verandahs, intricately detailed bay windows, Gothic buttresses, numerous finials, and a grand five-story tower. From the verandahs, there is a breathtaking view of the Hudson River and the Tappan Zee Bridge. The gray limestone building developed in two stages—the first as a house without the tower for General William Paulding, a commander in the War of 1812 and mayor of New York City. The second owner, George Merritt, a rich New York City merchant, bought the house in 1864 and rehired A. J. Davis to design an addition that almost doubled the size of the structure and added the distinctive tower that is topped by four turrets. Davis was an eminent furniture designer as well as architect, and he created about 150 pieces of stunning furniture for the house. Finally, the last residential use of the mansion was as the home of financier Jay Gould (1836-1892) and his family. Gould was the robber baron who swindled millions of dollars from the Erie Railroad and then tried to corner the gold market, causing the panic of 1869, known as Black Friday. Gould commuted to work aboard his 150-foot yacht from Lyndhurst, down the Hudson River to his office on Wall Street in lower Manhattan. The estate became a National Historic Landmark in 1966 and is operated today as a museum by the National Trust for Historic Preservation.

Above: The marble gazebo in the rose garden has a dome of filigreed iron.

Top left: Busts of the Marquis de Lafayette and George Washington adorn a hallway.

Top center: A male statue stands in front of the expansive porch at Lyndhurst.

Top right: The drawing room displays windows with delicate tracery, and the dramatic ceiling is lively and complex.

Above: The most opulent room in the house is the dining room with breath-taking Gothic Revival details.

Right: The second-floor library with its magnificent window was converted into an art gallery in 1865.

ANNANDALE-ON-HUDSON: BARD COLLEGE PERFORMING ARTS CENTER

*T*he prominent American architect, Frank Gehry, was 68 years old when he began the design of the $62 million Richard B. Fisher Center for the Performing Arts at Bard College in 1997. He was still working on the Guggenheim Museum in Bilbao, Spain at the time. He was 74 when the performing arts center was completed in 2003. It was Gehry's first design commission in the U.S. East. There are many similarities between the Bard College structure and the Bilbao museum, primarily their shimmering, undulating metal canopies, of stainless steel in the case of the performing arts center. Gehry maintains that he does not design at a drafting table; he designs through modeling, not drawing. The result is a building that some people consider flamboyant, because of its spectacular canopy with its exposed support system. Certainly there is nothing else like it in the Hudson Valley. The main theater seats 950; it features a movable concert shell made of Douglas fir that can accommodate a symphony orchestra, opera, dance, and drama. The acoustical shell and soundproofing were developed by Yasuhisa Toyota, a partner in Nagata Acoustics of Tokyo. A smaller theater seats 300, and under that massive reflective curving-metal canopy, there is still more room for studios and teaching rooms for drama and dance. The structure fits nicely into the 600-acre rural setting of Bard College with its heavily wooded campus and Catskill Mountains background.

ALBANY: NEW YORK STATE CAPITOL

*T*he booming industrial, commercial, financial, and agricultural growth brought about by the construction of the Erie Canal made New York the Empire State. It became apparent in the middle of the 19th century that the state needed a new capitol building to match its national preeminence. Its construction was a model of government inefficiency. It took 32 years to design and build and involved four separate architectural firms. Construction began in 1869 from plans drawn by architect Thomas Fuller (1823-1898), who chose to symbolize New York's great success with a structure of Italian Renaissance style. But after 7 years, the exterior walls were completed only to the second floor, and newly elected Lieutenant Governor William Dorsheimer was not satisfied. In 1876, he engaged high-powered new architects, Leopold Eidlitz (1823-1906) and Henry Hobson Richardson (1838-1886), along with the distinguished landscape architect Frederick Law Olmsted to design the capitol park. It was Richardson who dominated the final outcome of the grand building, which evolved into his distinguished Romanesque style. But Richardson and Eidlitz were not permitted to finish it either. When Grover Cleveland became governor, he reviewed the slow progress and enormous costs incurred for elaborately carved Scottish sandstone and granite, tons of Siena marble and Mexican onyx, and yards and yards of 23-carat gold leaf. He summarily dismissed Richardson and Eidlitz in 1883 and hired Isaac Perry (1822-1904) to complete the massive project. Despite its varied architectural styles, the capitol's exterior is definitely impressive, as is the peerless interior. Early critics called Richardson's Senate Chamber "the most beautiful room in the United States." When finally completed in 1899, three decades after its initiation, the building occupies a footprint that is 400 feet by 300 feet, covering four acres with Maine granite walls five feet thick. It is one of the last monumental, all-masonry buildings constructed in America, and it cost twice as much as the nation's Capitol in Washington, D.C.

Left: H. H. Richardson's Senate Chamber,
with interior details by Stanford White.

Above: Romanesque arches and columns abound in the wide hallways of the NYS Capitol.

Left: A detail shows the architectural motifs employed by architect H. H. Richardson.

Right: Wide heavy arches and clusters of squat columns enclose the atrium with a newly restored skylight.

KINDERHOOK: LINDENWALD

Kinderhook was the hometown of Martin Van Buren (1782-1862), who devoted his life to public service: New York senator, New York attorney general, U.S. senator, New York governor, U.S. secretary of state, U.S. ambassador to Great Britain, U.S. vice-president under Andrew Jackson, and eighth president of the United States (1837-1841). Van Buren was the first New Yorker to win the U.S. presidency. He was a strong leader, credited with dealing with the War of 1812, producing a new state constitution, overseeing the construction of the Erie Canal, expanding voting rights, inventing modern American national political parties, and while president, taking a firm antislavery stand. Seeking a place in his hometown in which to retire, he bought, in 1839, a Georgian style house that had been built in 1797. It came with 137 acres, which, as a gentleman farmer, he intended to manage. Van Buren's son, Smith Van Buren, requested that he come to live with his father and asked permission to make changes to the house in order to accommodate his family. With permission granted in 1838, Smith Van Buren engaged Richard Upjohn, architect of the masterpiece Trinity Church in New York City. The Italianate style was just coming into popularity, and that was what young Smith Van Buren wanted. Under Upjohn's plans, the house became a 36-room Italianate mansion with a portico added at the front entrance. Van Buren's household at Lindenwald was extensive with the enlarged family, servants, farm workers, and visiting friends and dignitaries seeking counsel from the great and wise leader. Van Buren used to call himself "O.K.," standing for "Old Kinderhook." The Democratic party's political club, the O.K. Club, used the expression in a slogan of endorsement for Van Buren in the election of 1840. And the expression stuck.

Above: The four-story brick tower was added when architect Richard Upjohn redesigned the house in Italianate style.

Below: The spacious library includes a bust of Martin Van Buren between two windows.

Right: The portico was added when the original Georgian house was updated to Italianate.

Above: A spectacular French wallpaper in the spacious entrance hall depicts a hunting scene. The southeast parlor is visible through the doorway.

Top right: The northeast parlor with its harp suggests its use as a music room.

Bottom right: A first-floor guest bedroom at Lindenwald features a canopied bed.

ALBANY: SCHUYLER MANSION

*P*hilip J. Schuyler (1733-1804) was the great-grandson of Philip Pieterse Schuyler, an early Dutch settler in New Netherland. The family was exceedingly rich and prominent, and by the time Philip J. Schuyler was 28 years old, he owned 125,000 acres of land in the Hudson Valley and was a successful businessman; at age 22, he became a provincial officer; he raised a company and was commissioned a captain in the French and Indian War, helping to expel the French from America; he married Catherine van Rensselaer from another wealthy Dutch family, and he was desirous of a new house. In 1761, he bought land on a bluff near the Hudson River and commenced building his mansion. On a trip to England that year, he purchased wallpapers, fabrics, carpets, silver, glassware, window glass, door and window hardware, and much more. Schuyler personally directed the construction and decoration of the interior. The result is one of the finest Georgian style houses in America. It is a five-bay, three-story house built of red brick. There is a marvelous Chinese Chippendale balustrade surrounding the double-hipped roof. The Federal style hexagonal vestibule was designed by Philip Hooker and added circa 1815. Although the house is basically English in style, Schuyler added some Dutch touches. The central hall is much wider than in Georgian structures and almost as wide as the rooms to either side. The hall is 20 feet wide in a house that is 63 feet wide; this is a Dutch tradition, which provides a large area for entertainment on the first floor and a central ballroom on the second. When it was completed in 1764, it was a surprising architectural statement in Albany, which at the time consisted largely of traditional Dutch architecture. In the Revolutionary War, Schuyler represented New York at the Continental Congress in Philadelphia and became a major general under George Washington. Schuyler called the house, "The Pastures," and he entertained a constant stream of distinguished guests there.

Right: The parlor is painted in a popular 18th-century color, yellow ochre.

Above: A picturesque scene covers the wall of the second-floor hall in the Schuyler Mansion.

Left: Bold wallpaper and carpet designs, typical of the period, decorate the study.

Right: A handsome staircase with Georgian style spindle designs sweeps upward from the wide entrance hall.

SCHENECTADY: NOTT MEMORIAL, UNION COLLEGE

*U*nion College can trace its beginnings to 1779, when 975 Schenectady residents signed a petition demanding the availability of higher education. In 1785, a nonsectarian academy was started. Finally, in 1795, a state Board of Regents charter, the first one to be issued in New York, established Union College, named for its union of people of different religious views. From its beginning, Union College had a liberal educational vision with emphasis on science, mathematics, and modern languages. It was the first liberal arts college in America to offer degrees in engineering. It also has the first architecturally designed campus in America, created by the French architect and landscape planner, J. J. Ramee, in 1814. The Nott Memorial, pictured here, is a 16-sided building that is the symbol of Union College and a National Historic Landmark. Its 1872 High Victorian Gothic design was by Edward Tuckerman Potter and memorializes Eliphalet Nott, president of the college from 1804 to 1866.

Left: The vast interior space rises 100 feet to the dome with auditorium space and a exhibition gallery on the second floor.

Above: The dome has 709 stained-glass windows arranged in bands of different colors.

Right: The structure is essentially a stone cylinder that is 89 feet in diameter.

SARATOGA SPRINGS: LINCOLN BATHS

*T*he Iroquois Indians named Saratoga Springs the "place of swift water" for all the "magical" springs that flowed from the ground. From General George Washington to Edgar Allan Poe, hundreds of thousands of visitors to Saratoga Springs have enjoyed the naturally carbonated spring water, which pushes up through limestone and shale absorbing various minerals to erupt as spring water with differing characteristics depending on the location of the spring. Today, there are free-flowing mineral springs throughout the city, each with distinctive taste and medicinal properties. There are also three operating mineral baths in the city (Lincoln Mineral Baths, The Crystal Spa, and Medbery Spa), all of them with the highest mineral content of any water in the world. The oldest mineral spa in Saratoga Springs is Lincoln Baths, which was originally built in 1911. That building burned in 1928 and was replaced by the current two-story white marble structure on South Broadway that opened in 1930. It was the largest mineral-bath building in the world and could provide 4,500 baths a day. It housed 252 bathtubs and 500 dressing rooms. There is a distinctive two-story portico supported by four stone columns with acanthus-leafed capitals. Above the architrave is a tableau with a central shield and two sculpted figures. Within the portico are three arched entrances.

SARATOGA SPRINGS: CONGRESS PARK AND CANFIELD CASINO

*R*ichard Albert Canfield (1855-1914), "Prince of Gamblers," with little formal education, became a highly successful gambler, who was a prolific reader and educated himself in his free time. He invested some of his winnings in art to the extent that he later became a friend of James McNeill Whistler, who painted his portrait. Canfield appeared in Saratoga Springs in 1893 and bought an impressive gambling establishment called the Club House that John Morrissey, ex-boxer and Tammany Hall "enforcer," had opened in 1870. Canfield spent over $1 million renovating the building and improving Congress Park that Morrissey had begun. By 1900, Canfield was the wealthiest gambler in the country. His casino patrons were a "Who's Who" of the world's rich and famous. Canfield managed the gambling establishment for 14 years. Then, antigambling laws made his operation difficult and in 1911 the village purchased Canfield Casino and made it a museum of Saratoga Springs history and part of Congress Park. The red-brick casino building reflects the Italianate style with a heavy projecting cornice held up by elaborate brackets and arched stone lintels on the first floor windows. The rich interior is filled with Victorian details like fancy chandeliers, monumental crown moldings, and period furniture by the famous New York City cabinetmaker, John Henry Belter. The most beautiful room in the casino was the restaurant added by Canfield in 1902. It has a barrel-vaulted ceiling covered with octagonal stained-glass skylights. Canfield also added the Italian Garden and much of the statuary in Congress Park. The most famous piece of sculpture in the park is a bronze figure, called the Spirit of Life, added in 1915. It was created by sculptor Daniel Chester French, who is most famous for his statue of President Abraham Lincoln in the Lincoln Memorial, Washington, D.C. There are three mineral springs in Congress Park: the Columbian, Congress, and Deer Park.

Left: Lincoln Baths is a two-story white marble structure that could provide 4,500 baths a day.

Top: The red-brick Italianate Canfield Casino is a history museum today.

Above: A classical stone baldachin is an architectural feature in one of the ponds of Congress Park.

SARATOGA SPRINGS: YADDO

Yaddo was the huge estate of Spencer and Katrina Trask. Besides a 550-acre wooded and hilly park dotted with lakes, there are 17 buildings on the Yaddo grounds including a mansion of 55 rooms that the Trasks built in 1891-1893. New Jersey architect William Halsey Wood (1855-1897) designed the stone mansion in Gothic Revival style. Wood was a brilliant, nationally known architect who primarily designed churches and created the Trask house design when he was 36 years old. He died just five years later at the age of 41 years. Spencer Trask, born in Brooklyn, became a highly successful New York City stockbroker and was publisher of the *Saratoga Union.* In 1889, in a rather unexplainable change of heart, he became a reformer and used his newspaper and political power to try to close down gambling in Saratoga Springs. When he and his wife died, the grand estate was left as a place where writers, painters, sculptors, printmakers, composers, and other artists could come to fulfill their creative talents. Yaddo is open to artists selected by an admissions committee of Yaddo Corporation. Carson McCullers, a Yaddo guest, dedicated "The Member of the Wedding" to Elizabeth Ames, Yaddo's executive director at the time. Truman Capote, James Baldwin, Katherine Anne Porter, Langston Hughes, Eudora Welty, Delmar Schwartz and critic Alfred Kazin all sharpened their writing skills at Yaddo. And painters like Jean Liberté and Joseph deMartini found inspiration for the subjects of their paintings at Yaddo.

Left: A classical stone and iron gate provides an entrance to a formal garden at Yaddo.

Top: A long colonnaded pergola provides a backdrop to one of Yaddo's many gardens.

Above: Yaddo is dotted with lakes, this one with fountains and sculpture.

SCHENECTADY: SCHENECTADY COUNTY HISTORICAL SOCIETY

*T*he Georgian Revival house at 32 Washington Avenue in Schenectady's Stockade District was built in 1895 and is an elegant house museum today. In 1662, villagers built a 10-foot-high stockade of pine logs around their compound to protect them from attacks by the Canadian French and their Indian allies, as France attempted to expand southward. In January 1690, 114 Frenchmen and 96 Indians left Montreal and began a 300-mile march to take over Schenectady. To the 400 residents in the stockade, it seemed unthinkable that anyone would march 300 miles through two feet of snow in bitter temperatures, so they neglected to lock their gates at night. But the French and Indians arrived unnoticed at 11 p.m. on February 8. At the signal of a bloodcurdling war whoop, they attacked every house simultaneously, breaking down doors with hatchets, shooting and axing every man, woman, and child that they encountered. Every house was set ablaze. The virtually unguarded outpost put up practically no resistance. The bloody massacre left 60 villagers dead, 27 carried off as captives, and others who perished from the cold in their flight from the stockade. Schenectady lay in ashes. But it was rebuilt with a unique collection of 17th- and 18th-century buildings, which are now protected by the first local historic preservation ordinance to be established in New York State. The Schenectady County Historical Society was a 19th-century addition to the particularly dense but handsome cluster of structures in the district.

ALBANY: DELAWARE AND HUDSON BUILDING

*M*arcus T. Reynolds (1869-1937) was a prolific Albany architect who designed in a variety of revival styles like Gothic, Baroque, Italian Renaissance, and Beaux Arts. As a young man, he spent a year-and-a-half in Europe studying classical architecture that inspired his future designs, which incorporated exuberant detailing and historical motifs that he imaginatively combined with contemporary materials and construction methods. One of the European buildings he studied was the 13th-century Gothic Cloth Hall in Ypres, Belgium. In 1914, that structure with its pinnacled tower became the inspiration for the architectural masterpiece of his career, the Delaware and Hudson Railroad Company Building. Lenore Loree, president of the D&H, asked Reynolds to design a new headquarters building for the railroad that had outgrown its current offices. The site was an area of old warehouses alongside the Hudson River, which had been proposed for redevelopment. Reynolds designed a monumental, 660-foot-long structure of limestone and cast-stone in Flemish Revival style. The project also

included headquarters for the *Albany Evening Journal* to be housed in an adjoining building at the south end of the Delaware and Hudson structure. The focal point of the long curving building is a 13-story Gothic tower with a thin spire topped by a copper weathervane in the shape of the ship, *Half Moon,* in which explorer Henry Hudson discovered the navigable limit of the Hudson River, now Albany. The Gothic details throughout the building complex are numerous and delightful. Besides the expected Gothic turrets and steeply peaked windows and gables, there are cast-stone Gothic symbols, as well as historic representations, like the beaver, symbolizing the fur trade, which was the original reason for Dutch settlement here. On the Albany Evening Journal building, there are printers' marks in decorative panels. The Journal stopped publication in 1926, and the railroad vacated in 1974. By 1978, the huge complex was converted to the State University of New York Central Administration Headquarters, with a penthouse residence in the Journal tower for the university chancellor.

ESSEX: ESSEX INN

*T*he entire village of Essex, with its carefully preserved 19th-century structures of wood, brick, and stone, is listed in the National Register of Historic Places. It possesses one of the best collections of Federal and Greek Revival architecture in the state. The village, located on the shore of Lake Champlain, was founded in 1765 and produced the wealth to build all of its fine buildings primarily from stone quarries, shipping, and shipyards. One significant Federal style building that is open to the public is the Essex Inn, built in 1810 and situated in the center of the small village. It is a two-story, wood-frame structure with a colonnaded porch on both the first and second floors across the entire long width of the façade. The columns, painted white like the remaining wood trim on the building, are slender, Doric in style, and tall, being two stories high. Despite its impressive length on Main Street, the inn is surprisingly narrow in depth, just one room and hallway deep.

Opposite: The façade of the Essex Inn includes a full-length, two-story colonnaded porch.

Left: The Essex library, with its symmetrical façade, has balconies on the second and third floors.

Above: The Essex harbor on Lake Champlain where the ferry to Vermont docks.

*Top: Battlements of Fort Ticonderoga face
Lake Champlain to the south.*

*Above and right: Barracks at the fort are
built of limestone and form a quadrangle.*

TICONDEROGA: FORT TICONDEROGA

*F*ort Ticonderoga is a 2,200-acre site today; it played strategic and critical roles in the control of the Champlain Valley by the French, British, and Americans. The French built the first fort in 1755 and successfully defended it on July 8, 1758, in the Battle of Carillon (the name of the fort at the time) in the French and Indian War. It was the greatest French victory of that war, but they finally lost the fort to the British in 1759. In a surprise predawn attack on May 10, 1775, Ethan Allen, Benedict Arnold, and the Green Mountain Boys captured the fort from the British, making this the first American victory in the Revolutionary War. Two years later, the British under General John Burgoyne recaptured the fort in July 1777, and British forces held it to the end of the war. It was the British who named the fort, "Ticonderoga," a Mohawk Indian word meaning "the land between two waters," which aptly describes the fort's position between Lakes George and Champlain. The first fort was built of two parallel rows of logs that were reinforced with packed earth in between the logs, which gave the walls great strength. Later, these walls were upgraded to limestone quarried on site. The stone walls of the fortress are configured in a star shape, making it possible to repel attacks from any direction. The barracks for the officers and soldiers are two stories high, built of limestone, and form a quadrangle. The space within becomes a parade ground. On that fateful predawn morning in 1775, Allen, Arnold, and their small band of colonials, who called themselves the Green Mountain Boys, entered Fort Ticonderoga through an unlocked gate. Although a British sentry fired at them, it was a misfire, and Allen's men managed to enter the quadrangle where the most distant building was the officers' quarters. They climbed an outdoor wooden staircase to a second-floor wood balcony, and entered the first door on the left, which was the commandant's quarters. The startled British commandant, still in bed, surrendered the garrison.

NEWCOMB: CAMP SANTANONI

*T*oday, there are several dozen rustic estates in the Adirondacks that have become known as "Great Camps." These typically were built for a single family; are located on the water; constructed of indigenous, natural materials; have separate buildings, each with a specific function, and usually have some degree of self-sufficiency in the way of a farm operation. Camp Santanoni was built beginning in 1892 for Robert C. Pruyn, a prominent Albany banker and businessman. It was the first camp to be designed by a professional architect, Robert H. Robertson (1849-1914). Like the other Great Camps, it was built beside a lake, in this case, Newcomb Lake. It took 1,500 native spruce trees, harvested on the 12,900-acre estate itself, to build the 15,000-square-foot main lodge, which is a grouping of six separate buildings all connected by a common roof-and-porch system. The main living area has a two-story-high ceiling covered with hand-hewn wood beams. Giant fieldstone fireplaces provide heat in the mountain climate, and decorative half-log patterns cover the walls and doors. There are more than 45 buildings constructed of indigenous wood and stone, including a boathouse, lakeside studio, gatehouse, and farm buildings. The main lodge is truly remote, being five miles through the woods from the Gate Lodge parking area. Each building has its separate function, hence such specific-use structures as the stone creamery, workshop, chicken house, kennels, smoke house, root cellar, wagon sheds, etc. The farm supplied the camp with milk, meat, vegetables, fruit, and eggs. In fact, the farm had surpluses that it sold in the surrounding community. Pruyn was a well known person and many distinguished people visited Santanoni, two frequent visitors being Theodore Roosevelt and James Fenimore Cooper, Jr. Today, the huge estate is owned by the State of New York and is open to the public. In 1901, U.S. Vice-President Theodore Roosevelt was vacationing at Camp Santanoni when he learned that President McKinley had been shot at the Pan-American Exposition in Buffalo.

A huge stone fireplace heats the interior of the main lodge.

Above: A covered walkway connects two camp buildings.

Top: The stone entrance gate is five miles from the main lodge.

Right: The porch of the main lodge at Camp Santanoni.

NORTH ELBA: JOHN BROWN FARM

John Brown (1800-1859) was a man with a moral vision and the courage and determination to pursue it. At a time when America was tolerant of slavery, he became one of the principal opponents to its continuance and a significant proponent of equality for all of our country's citizens. His view was that slavery would cease only if someone ended it, and he was determined to be involved in that goal. In 1849, John Brown established his farm on John Brown Road, near Lake Placid. His idea was to help free-born blacks and runaway slaves to homestead in the vast unsettled Adirondacks. Farming conditions in the rugged countryside and harsh winter weather, however, proved to be too much to overcome. Brown eventually had 20 children by two wives, the first wife died in childbirth. On May 24, 1856, Brown decided to retaliate against the violence of pro-slave mobs in Kansas. He, along with five of his sons and other abolitionists, armed themselves with

swords and, pretending to be travelers seeking directions, lured pro-slavery leaders out of their homes and massacred them. Five men were murdered. Brown was never arrested for the killings, and when he returned back East, he was hailed a hero and received the backing of a group of wealthy abolitionists known as the Secret Six. They planned a raid on the Federal arsenal at Harper's Ferry, Virginia, intending to capture weapons in order to launch a slave insurrection. The seizure of the arsenal took place on October 16, 1859. Colonel Robert E. Lee, then in the U.S. Army, and his Marines stormed the arsenal and captured Brown, who was tried for insurrection, treason, and murder. He was convicted and hanged in Charlestown, Virginia. His martyrdom was commemorated with the song, "The Battle Hymn of the Republic." Brown's body, as well as those of other family members, is buried at his Adirondack farm, a New York State Historic Site.

Left: An interior view of John Brown's modest Adirondack wood-frame house.

RAQUETTE LAKE: CAMP SAGAMORE

*O*ne of the pioneers and the founder of the rustic style associated with the Adirondacks was William West Durant (1850-1934). His first venture was Camp Pine Knot built in 1879. He combined the rustic qualities of Adirondack log cabins with the decorative gracefulness and long, low lines of Swiss chalets that he had admired on a trip to Switzerland. Thus began the distinctive type of Adirondack architecture, copied and embellished ever since throughout the region. From 1895 to 1897, Durant designed and built his third camp, his masterpiece, Camp Sagamore, and sold it in 1901 to Alfred Gwynne Vanderbilt, Sr. (1877-1915), the wealthiest man in America, having inherited the bulk of the $80 million Vanderbilt fortune. He was just 18 years old. The three-story main lodge on the 1,526-acre estate, overlooking the lake, had indoor plumbing with hot and cold running water, a sewer and septic system, gaslights, and huge stone fireplaces. The beams in the main lodge are full-length tree trunks from the tallest trees on the estate. Although the camp buildings were made to look like log structures, they are really standard wood-frame construction with half-log façades. The door to the main lodge resembles a medieval castle entrance with heavy iron hinges and large locks requiring giant forged keys. The dining hall soon became too small for Sagamore entertaining, and an expansion in 1924 accommodated 70 people who arrived for Christmas dinner. The complex also includes rustic guest cottages, boathouse, pump house, laundry, icehouse, casino/playhouse, bowling alley with a loop-de-loop ball return, carriage house, workshops, blacksmith shop, and more. On May 4, 1915, Alfred Vanderbilt was returning from Europe on the Lusitania, which was sunk by a German torpedo. As the ship sank, Alfred gave his life vest to a woman with a child, who lived to report his heroic act. His last words were, "Come and let us save the kiddies." He was 38 years old. His wife, Margaret, continued to live at Sagamore every summer until 1954, when she gave the camp to Syracuse University. It is now a National Historic Landmark owned by the Sagamore Institute.

Left: Exterior walls of Camp Sagamore buildings were faced in birch bark and decoratively patterned split logs.

Top: The boathouse at Camp Sagamore was both an important facility and popular place.

Above: With a roof overhead, the Sagamore bowling alley was protected, yet open on the sides to the fresh mountain air.

WESTPORT TRAIN STATION

*I*n 1876, the Delaware and Hudson Railroad built the Westport Train Station on the rail line that connected east coast U.S. cities with Montreal, Canada. Westport faces Lake Champlain with the high peaks of the Adirondacks to the west and is a popular tourist destination. The depot at 6705 Main Street in Westport is still a stop on the Amtrak Adirondack line. But it is much more than a train station today. The Westport Historical Society acquired the picturesque structure in 1974 and began a long-term restoration. Today, there is a Tourist Information Center, a museum of Westport and railroad historic artifacts, an art gallery displaying the works of area artists and craftsmen, and, most notably, a professional theatre company. The old freight room was renovated to establish the 137-seat Depot Theatre. The lobby of the theatre serves several purposes: theater entrance, depot waiting room, and art gallery. The unique broad slate roof—with gently sloping conical elements, one of which is topped by a cupola—underwent a complete replacement in 1998 of the century-old slates with new gray-green slate from Vermont, just across the lake. This prominent roof can be seen from a considerable distance in the Champlain Valley corridor. And the view from the depot itself is spectacular, with beautiful Lake Champlain in front of the depot and the high peaks to the back.

TICONDEROGA: HANCOCK HOUSE

*H*orace Augustus Moses was a native of Ticonderoga who consolidated several paper mills to create Strathmore Paper Company. In returning some of his enormous wealth to his hometown, he decided to build a museum and library for Ticonderoga. He selected to construct a replica of the famous Hancock House on Beacon Street in Boston, which had been demolished in 1863. John Hancock (1737-1793) was orphaned as a child and adopted by his wealthy childless uncle, Thomas Hancock, who built the Hancock mansion on Beacon Street in 1737, the year John Hancock was born. John inherited the house and his uncle's wealth when Thomas died in 1763. John's lifelong home was one of the finest Colonial mansions and a splendid example of Georgian style architecture. He became a prominent Boston merchant and president of the Continental Congress from 1775 to 1777. John Hancock was the very first congressman to sign the Declaration of Independence. His bold signature on the document was followed by all of the other members, thereby "adding their John Hancocks" to the historic document. Before the Boston house was demolished in 1863, the architect John Sturgis made carefully measured drawings, and these were available for Moses to replicate. The copy would also be fireproof, like the original. The same Weymouth granite was used, and the interior details are precisely those of the earlier house. Even the paint colors, primarily a sophisticated gray on the walls, reflect the refined taste of 18th-century architecture. So here, in a different location, but with meticulous attention to every detail, the historic John Hancock Mansion in Boston was resurrected in 1926. Moses gave his replicated Hancock House to the New York State Historical Association, which established a museum and library in the building and used it as the association's headquarters until they were moved to Cooperstown. Today, the Ticonderoga Historical Society manages this important house museum and research library under the auspices of the NYSHA.

CROWN POINT: LIGHTHOUSE/CHAMPLAIN MEMORIAL

W hen the French occupied this area and built a fort here around 1737, they erected a windmill on the current lighthouse site. But they blew up the windmill with gunpowder in 1759 when they abandoned the fort to the British. When peaceful times arrived in the 1800s and commercial traffic was heavy on Lake Champlain, it became apparent that a lighthouse was needed here to guide boats at this narrow point in the lake. The first lighthouse built in 1858 was a 55-foot-high, octagonal limestone tower attached to a wooden keeper's cottage. The lantern room beamed its Fresnel-lens light through trapezoidal windowpanes. For 50 years, this light, which was visible for 15 miles, provided faithful service. Then in 1910, which was the tricentennial of the discovery of the lake by Samuel de Champlain (1567-1635), it was determined that a memorial to the great explorer should be erected on the site. A clever solution kept the lighthouse intact and operating. A grand, classical memorial was built around the cylindrical light-

house shaft and spiral staircase. A high circular base was constructed of granite from Fox Island, Maine. Above it, eight granite Doric columns support the ornate circular cornice and parapet. On a platform facing the lake, there are bronze statues of Champlain flanked by an American Indian and a French sailor. The sculpture was created by the American artist Carl Heber. U.S. President William H. Taft dedicated the memorial in 1912, and a French delegation presented a bronze bas relief medallion created by Auguste Rodin, which is mounted below the sculpture of Champlain. The Crown Point State Historic Site also contains the remains of a 1734 French fort, which was a four-story stone octagon with cannons poking through the 12-foot-thick walls on all four stories. After 1759, the British built their own fort here, which was the largest British stronghold in the American colonies. Today, French and British flags fly peacefully over the ruins of their separate fortresses.

Above: The bridge across Lake Champlain from Crown Point, New York, to Chimney Point, Vermont.

Left: The Crown Point lighthouse is encased by the Samuel de Champlain Memorial.

DANUBE: HERKIMER HOME

*T*wo miles east of Little Falls on the south side of the Mohawk River and near the original Erie Canal is Herkimer Home, built circa 1750 for Brigadier General Nicholas Herkimer. It is a Georgian style, gambrel-roofed house built of brick imported from Holland. It was General Herkimer who led the militia in the Revolutionary War Battle of Oriskany on August 6, 1777. He was leading 800 militiamen to recapture Fort Stanwix in Rome. Herkimer initially opposed advancing further until he could get reinforcements to face what he considered overwhelming British forces, who might set an ambush. His officers, however, were eager to proceed and argued so fiercely that Herkimer relented. Sure enough, the British staged an ambuscade, and one of the bloodiest battles of the war ensued. The Americans stood their ground thereby preventing British reinforcements from reaching the Hudson River Valley, where combined efforts of British forces from the west and east might have changed the war's outcome. In the course of the fighting, General Herkimer was seriously wounded in one leg but continued to direct his militia until the British and the Indians retreated. He was taken to his home where his leg was amputated. Ten days after the battle he died from a hemorrhage caused by the amputation. The general was buried on a knoll just a short distance from his residence.

Left: A first-floor bedroom at Herkimer Home is set up for breakfast at a skirted table.

Overleaf: The dining room of General Nicholas Herkimer's house is illuminated by 12-over-12, double-hung windows.

Top: The Cooperstown Public Library is fronted by a colonnaded porch across the wide façade.

Above: Two views of the Farmers' Museum in Cooperstown, a 19th-century village with artisans displaying their trades, heritage gardens, and farmstead animals.

COOPERSTOWN: FENIMORE ART MUSEUM

*T*he elegant neo-Georgian mansion on the shore of Otsego Lake was built in 1932 and called Fenimore House, named for James Fenimore Cooper (1789-1851), whose country house once stood on this site. James Fenimore Cooper, America's first great novelist, carries the surnames of both his parents, William Cooper and Elizabeth Fenimore. In 1944, Fenimore House became the headquarters of the New York State Historical Association when Stephen Carlton Clark, heir to a Singer Sewing Machine Company fortune and prominent art collector, presented Fenimore House, which he owned, to the association. Today, with several additions added over the years, it is the Fenimore Art Museum, housing the vast collection of American art of the New York State Historical Association. As a youth, James Fenimore Cooper roamed the primeval forest surrounding this estate and developed a love for nature that influenced his later writings. Cooper was the son of Quaker parents. His father, Judge William Cooper, was a wealthy landowner who founded Cooperstown in 1790. When Cooper was 13 years old, he was sent to Yale University, but was expelled in his junior year for getting a donkey to sit in the chair of a particular professor. Nonetheless, he soon became a world-famous author of many novels, including *The Leatherstocking Tales,* which consist of *The Deerslayer, Last of the Mohicans, The Pathfinder, The Prairie,* and *The Pioneers.* Cooper died in Cooperstown on September 14, 1851, and is buried in the Cooper family plot located behind the Old Episcopal Church.

UTICA: UNION STATION

*O*utside of New York City, the only train station in New York State that reflects the grandeur and opulence of the golden age of railroading is Union Station in Utica. In fact, it has few peers in our country. It even sits on an appropriately historic site: the location was a 19th-century stagecoach stop at the convenient point for fording the Mohawk River. Also, an earlier train station of Greek Revival style was built here in 1836. Another railroad station replaced it and was erected on the site in 1869. Finally, the current Union Station was constructed in 1914. Plans for the monumental Beaux Arts style structure were created by the architectural firm of Stem & Fellheimer. The granite and brick building with its classical detailing is three stories high with the upper two floors used as railroad offices. The main-floor interior, with its wonderful barrel-vaulted and coffered ceilings and marble columns quarried in Vermont, create a waiting room that reflects the true glory of train travel in the past. The walls are finished in marble, and there is a terrazzo floor. Handsome oak benches provide seating for waiting travelers. For Utica, the construction of Union Station in 1914 was the culmination of a series of public works in the city, including relocating the Mohawk River to eliminate flooding.

UTICA: FOUNTAIN ELMS

*F*ountain Elms, part of the Museum of Art, Munson-Williams-Proctor Arts Institute in Utica, is a brick Italianate house designed by Albany architect, William L. Woolett, Jr., for Alfred Munson, who made a gift of it to his daughter, Helen, and son-in-law, James Watson Williams. Fountain Elms received its name from the fountain and two elm trees in the front yard. The house, built between 1850-1852, has a notable, restored interior with the four first-floor rooms elegantly furnished in 1850s style. It is now a house museum open to the public. One June 5, 1823, Alfred Munson—a six-foot, lean, handsome young man of 30 years— arrived in Utica with his new bride, Elizabeth. Alfred had sold his share of the family farm, grist mill, and sawmill for $2900 and was striking out on his own. Knowing a little about milling from his family's business in Connecticut, he began to make high-quality buhr millstones, which he marketed up and down the Erie Canal. He invested in canal and lake boats and later in railroads, as well as land and iron works, amassing a fortune that led him to develop steam mills, fired by Pennsylvania coal that was inexpensively available on the Chenango Canal. His steam mills made Utica the knit-goods center of the world. Ill for many years with tuberculosis, Munson died in 1855 at the age of 62 years. Part of his enormous fortune started the Munson-Williams-Proctor Arts Institute.

UTICA: STANLEY THEATER

*T*he great movie palace of central New York State is the
Stanley Theater in Utica. It was a premier showplace when it
opened on September 10, 1928, and it still is today. The movie
house was named in memory of Stanley V. Mastbaum, who was
the founder and president of the Stanley Company of America,
which was the largest operator of motion picture theaters in
America. In the 1920s, they owned more than 400 theaters in the
United States and Canada. After Stanley's death, the company was
managed by his brother, Jules Mastbaum. The Stanley Theater was
designed by Thomas Lamb, one of the most prolific theater architects in the country in the early part of the 20th century. The
building incorporates a variety of architectural styles—the principal
ones being Baroque, Moorish, and Art Deco. Theater experts dub
it "Mexican Baroque." The exterior, which is clad in terra cotta and
tile, displays Mexican influence, while the lavish Baroque interior
is filled with countless yards of gold leaf, as well as lions, Indian
faces, angels, and cherubs. Moorish inspiration is suggested in
the ceiling, which is filled with twinkling stars, and the twisted
columns, which flank the stage. The draperies covering the organ
pipes are Art Deco in treatment. On that opening evening in 1928,
over 3,500 people arrived to see the movie, *Ramona* starring
Dolores Del Rio and Warner Baxter, but what overwhelmed them
was the incredible theater itself. It takes 230,445 watts to turn on
the lights in the Stanley. There are 4,500 bulbs ranging in size
from 15 watts to 500 watts. The marquee uses 726 15-watt bulbs
and 510 25-watt bulbs. The theater cost $1.5 million dollars to
build in 1928, but when it was restored in 1974, the cost was
over $5.5 million.

*Top: Twisted columns flank the ornate
stage of the Stanley Theater.*

*Above: An ornate iron balustrade
surrounds the staircase on the balcony
lobby.*

*Overleaf: The lavish interior of the
Stanley Theater in Utica holds more
than 3,500 people.*

ONEIDA: ONEIDA COMMUNITY MANSION HOUSE

*J*ohn Humphrey Noyes and his followers, known as the Oneida
Perfectionists, established their Oneida Community in 1848.
Hundreds of converts were attracted to his hardworking, patriarchal
cooperative that abandoned private ownership, whether of worldly
goods or wives, and practiced birth control by male continence.
Noyes' members were Christian communists sharing everything
with each other and loving each other, not in pairs but commu-
nally. He felt such an experimental community would be tolerated
in the free air of New York State. It was. He went so far as to
institute a system of breeding to produce new generations of
particularly vigorous and intelligent people by selecting couples,
including himself, obviously, and a number of young women, to
procreate. In 1852, the society began the construction of a massive,
rambling U-shaped Victorian home built in a number of stages until
it was completed in 1914. The Second Empire style, multipurpose
mansion is constructed of red brick with mansard roofs clad in
decorative slate shingles. Most of the structure is three stories high
with a square four-story tower. One of the manufacturing efforts
of the industrious Oneida Community was the production of silver
tableware. The radical communal society was dissolved in 1881,
but Oneida Limited continues to this day and is synonymous with
refined dining and quality tableware. The house was designated a
National Historic Landmark in 1965.

Right: The auditorium, although built in
Victorian times, displays the sparseness
of Shaker communities, with its simple
benches and subdued decoration.

JOHNSTOWN: SIR WILLIAM JOHNSON HALL

Sir William Johnson (1715-1774) was the founder of Johnstown, Superintendent of Indian Affairs for Great Britain, major general of the British army, colonel of Six Nations, and leader of the settlement of the Mohawk River Valley. He came to America from Ireland in 1732 to manage the vast land holdings in the Mohawk Valley of his uncle, Sir Peter Warren. He became a leading political figure in the colony, won the confidence and friendship of the Mohawk Indians and the Iroquois Confederacy, and was appointed colonel of the frontier militia during the French and Indian wars. With help from the friendly Indians, he won major victories for the English and was summoned to England to be knighted and awarded a baronetcy. Along the way, he acquired wealth as well as title, and bought a large tract of land in which he founded Johnstown, which he named for his son, John. It was here that Sir William, in 1763, decided to build his mansion, a large Georgian style frame residence. He hired a noted Boston carpenter, Samuel Fuller, to construct the wooden house, which was scored to look like stone. Originally, the estate included formal gardens, a mill, blacksmith shop, Indian store, barns, and servants' housing. Two stone block houses flank the mansion itself. An early visitor to the baronial estate wrote, "Off the river about 14 miles back, Sir William Johnson has made a new Settlement and has built a very comfortable house, having a Good Garden and field, all cleared in an Absolute Forest. At this place he is generally crowded with Indians, mostly of the 5 Nations." Johnson Hall was designated a National Historic Landmark in 1960.

Left: The gun rack just inside the entrance door is a reminder that this was dangerous territory in the 1700s.

Right: Sir William Johnson's portrait and Indian artifacts that he loved to collect hang above the fireplace in the blue parlor, which is set up here for dining.

Above: In a bedroom on the second floor, the bed was fitted with a fabric canopy to reduce drafts.

Left: Wide central hallways were typical in mansions of the 1700s as is evident in this main-floor hall. Animal hides on the wall represented the principal export product at the time.

Opposite: On a table in a first-floor bedroom beneath the wall barometer is a wig stand, with wig.

SPRINGFIELD: HYDE HALL

When building a great mansion, it always helps to have had a great grandfather who was lieutenant governor of the British Province of New York from 1703 to 1743 and who amassed an estate of 120,000 acres of New York State land, which ended up being left to his eight-year-old great grandson in 1777. That descendant of the first George Clarke was also named George Clarke (1768-1835). When the great grandson decided to leave England and emigrate to America to claim his inheritance, he was 38 years old. He selected a site central to his vast land holdings on a bluff on the northeastern shore of Otsego Lake near Cooperstown with a magnificent view and over the next 18 years from 1817 to 1835 built one of the great houses in America. He commissioned the most prominent New York State architect of the time, Philip Hooker of Albany, to design a 50-room neo-classical limestone country house that would remind him of his homeland, England. Hooker had designed such sizable structures as the original New York State Capitol, Albany City Hall, Albany Academy, and Hamilton College chapel. He had also designed many residences but nothing as grand, as monumental as Hyde Hall. It is the largest domestic structure built in America between the Revolution and the Civil War. There is a Doric Greek Revival portico with a balcony surrounded by a wrought-iron railing. Extensive wings, including a chapel, extend from the main building. The interior displays ornate friezes, elegant fireplaces, and other elaborate interior finishes. The main stairwell is housed in a three-story rounded tower; there is a central enclosed stone-paved courtyard. But George Clarke never truly lived in his dream house; he died in 1835 before the innovative central heating system was fully installed. Hyde Hall is a National Historic Landmark and a New York State Historic Site.

Left: After dinner, the men retreated to the Men's Parlor, with its bright red walls, for brandy and cigars.

135

Left: A dramatic curved three-story staircase hugs a semicircular wall.

Top: After dinner at Hyde Hall, the women retreated to the Women's Parlor for (would you guess?) gossip.

Above: A covered porch overlooks Otsego Lake.

SHARON SPRINGS: AMERICAN HOTEL

Sharon Springs, with a year-round population of 550, is unlike other New York State villages. It is renowned for its interesting and unique architecture. Back in the years from the 1860s to the mid-1940s, it was internationally famous as a health spa. It has 180 buildings listed in the National Register of Historic Places. They include classical temples, bathhouses, 60 rambling hotels, and charming Victorian houses. The multiple springs here are particularly special. The village is known for its magnesium water, its iron-rich water, its sulfur water, and its "bluestone" water for healing the eyes—all in one little village. It once drew 10,000 resort visitors in the summer. The Vanderbilts and the Roosevelts regularly stayed here. President Ulysses S. Grant took the waters here. And Oscar Wilde lectured in Sharon Springs. So, what happened? Well, besides a decline in the popularity of mineral-water spas, there came Saratoga Springs, which was not just a spa, but also a summer resort for horse racing and gambling, and became the preferred gathering spot for New York's society. Sharon Springs, however, is undergoing rejuvenation. One of the prominent renovations is the American Hotel, an 1847 Greek Revival structure with 26 rooms that had closed in the 1950s. Nicolas M. LaRue, founder of the American Hotel, and his descendants aimed to "furnish superior accommodations at reasonable rates," also providing a table "abundantly supplied with delicacies fresh and in season." The hotel is a stately white, clapboard building with a two-story porch along the entire façade and a 65-seat restaurant serving "delicacies fresh and in season."

Above: A historic one-room schoolhouse has separate entrances for boys and girls.

Right: Imperial Baths is one of several mineral-springs bathhouses in Sharon Springs.

138

ALEXANDRIA BAY: BOLDT CASTLE

George C. Boldt (1852-1916) was the owner of the Bellevue-Stratford Hotel in Philadelphia and the proprietor of the Waldorf-Astoria Hotel in New York City. He purchased a five-acre island in the St. Lawrence River, reconfigured the island into a more perfect heart shape by constructing a 500-foot gently curving lagoon, called it Heart Island, and began the construction of a complex of buildings including a 120-room mansion—all to express his love and devotion to his wife, Louise. The estate was designed in a mixture of medieval and Victorian styles by the Philadelphia architectural firm of W.D. Hewitt and G.W. Hewitt. Boldt engaged 300 stonemasons, carpenters, and artists to construct the grandiose six-story stone residence, reminiscent of Rhineland castles in his native Germany, with towers, spires, turrets, steep gables, candle-snuffer roofs, crenellations, finials, and massive chimneys. The complex included 10 additional ornate medieval buildings, as well as tunnels, drawbridge, dovecote, and Italian gardens. A huge, 64-foot-high yacht house was erected on neighboring Wellesley Island. When work was 90 percent complete in 1904, Louise suddenly died. Heartbroken, Boldt abandoned the project and never returned to Heart Island. He died in 1916, a shattered man. The Thousand Islands Bridge Authority acquired the estate in 1977 and undertook a restoration that has so far cost $12 million. An entry hall with a grand staircase receives daylight from a skylighted central dome four stories above. A number of meticulously reno-vated rooms are open to the public, including the reception room, billiard room, and dining room. These rooms display elaborate plasterwork and fine oak paneling, marble fireplaces, Louis XV-style furniture, and Boldt family china and silverware.

Left: The Shingle style Yacht House rises 64 feet above the water and has slips 128 feet long to accommodate the family's three yachts and their 110-foot, two-story houseboat.

Top: The Boldt Castle complex with a dozen medieval-style buildings occupied a five-acre island in the St. Lawrence River.

Above: The Power House and Clock Tower, resembling a stone medieval fortress, provided electricity to the island complex.

Above: The boat livery and public docks were rebuilt to their original 1912 appearance.

Left: Cottages in the park have fanciful cutout and lathe-turned architectural details.

Below: The community library is a charming, modest Greek Revival frame building.

WELLESLEY ISLAND, THOUSAND ISLAND PARK: BOAT LIVERY AND PUBLIC DOCKS

*A*t the end of St. Lawrence Avenue in Thousand Island Park are the community's main dock and pavilion, the Park's window on the river. Rehabilitated to its 1912 appearance, the pavilion is an important landmark on the St. Lawrence River. The entire community of Thousand Island Park was listed in the National Register of Historic Places in 1982.

WELLESLEY ISLAND, THOUSAND ISLAND PARK: LIBRARY

*I*n 1875, the Rev. John F. Dayan, caught up in the religious fervor of the time, formed a Methodist summer community on the southwestern tip of Wellesley Island in the St. Lawrence River. It was a place where families could receive spiritual and physical renewal during summer months. Vacationers would set up tents or build cottages to participate in the nonsectarian activities. By 1894, the place had added hotel accommodations in addition to some 500 to 600 cottages in the park. The Depression and its economic hardships reduced the number of cottages to 320 in the mid-1950s. An energetic restoration effort occurred on the 100th anniversary of the park in 1975, with renovation of the existing 19th-century cottages with all of their charm and gingerbread. Here in the 145-acre site are Gothic Revival, Queen Anne, Eastlake, Stick style, Shingle style, and newer frame cottages in Bungalow style, most of them built between 1875 and 1920. The community has abandoned most of its religious aspects today, but the beautiful, idyllic setting and charming architecture still minister to the psyche. Here, the little Greek Revival library provides summer reading for residents.

CLAYTON: LA DUCHESSE HOUSEBOAT

When George C. Boldt built his magnificent Boldt Castle on Heart Island in the Thousand Islands, he also undertook the construction of a houseboat. Although 90 percent complete, the houseboat was left to deteriorate in its berth in the yacht house when Boldt abandoned the entire property in 1904. Edward J. Noble bought the estate, including the boats, in 1924. The houseboat was partially submerged when Andrew McNally IV, chairman of Rand McNally & Company, bought it in 1943 from his friend, Ed Noble, for $1 with a promise to remove it from the yacht house. McNally completely restored the 110-foot, two-story houseboat and spent summers on it until he died at age 92 in 2001. He bequeathed *La Duchesse* to the Antique Boat Museum in Clayton,

where it is open to the public as part of the boat museum. La Duchesse is no ordinary houseboat. With 4,000 square feet, it is a Gilded Age mansion on a raft. There are two working fireplaces; the one in the formal dining room has shells, starfish, and sea serpents carved into the brass mantelpiece. The drawing room is finished in dark mahogany with Ionic pilasters, a beamed ceiling, and a second fireplace. There are eight staterooms, a galley, and crew quarters. On the upper level, there is an expansive open deck and a salon, with a dance floor that is 18 feet by 50 feet with no columns or obstructions. There is gold-leaf stenciling on the ceiling and a coffered stained-glass skylight. Another amenity is a white mahogany Steinway piano.

Top left: The 4,000-square-foot, two-story La Duchesse houseboat.

Above left: The drawing room in dark mahogany.

Above: The dance floor in the salon is 50 feet long.

Right: The master bedroom is one of eight staterooms.

Far right: The white mahogany Steinway piano is illuminated by a stained-glass skylight.

CLAYTON: ANTIQUE BOAT MUSEUM

*T*he home for *La Duchesse* is the Antique Boat Museum in Clayton, where more than 200 antique boats form what Joe Gibbins of *Nautical Quarterly* called "the largest and most impressive collection of inland recreational boats in the world." In six major buildings and a number of docks, the collection of wooden antique boats includes skiffs, canoes, sailboats, early powerboats, launches, runabouts, vintage raceboats, speedboats, luxury motor yachts, and the peerless *La Duchesse* houseboat.

Above and right: Antique boats are displayed in six major buildings.

Opposite page, clockwise from top left: Front porch of the Commandant's House in Sackets Harbor; the Lieutenant's House as seen from the back porch of the Commandant's House; Sackets Harbor on Lake Ontario with one of the old U.S. Naval Station buildings, now part of the museum complex.

SACKETS HARBOR: COMMANDANT'S HOUSE

*T*he Sackets Harbor Naval Station where many American warships were constructed was protected by Fort Tompkins. In the War of 1812, the British were intent on destroying the navy yard and the ship under construction, the *General Pike*. In order to accomplish this, they needed to take the fort. Americans held their ground during a surprise attack by the British on May 29, 1813. Guns at the fort continued firing, despite the heat and smoke from the burning barracks and storehouses that the British destroyed. Americans in the fort were determined not to be dislodged from the blockhouse and fought until the British finally retreated. Fort Tompkins, however decimated, was never taken. During the war, eight warships were built and launched at Sackets Harbor. After the war, Sackets Harbor continued as a naval station, and in 1847, a new house for the commandant was built. The Greek Revival house was completed in 1848. The rear façade depicted is almost identical to the front elevation except for a central entrance door on the front. Full-length porches on both the first and second

floors extend along the front and back sides of the house. One attractive feature is the decorative embellishments to the porches. The porch railings, open columns, and roof cresting all incorporate Greek tracery designs. If this house were in the South, these decorative elements would all be made of cast iron. Here, they are carved wood, making them particularly special. The house appears deceptively small, but it contains four floors of living space. The basement level has its own side entrance and includes a large passage and work area (primarily for laundry activities), furnace room, servants' dining room, storage room, and kitchen. The first floor includes an entrance hall, parlor, dining room, family room and library, pantry, and stairs to the second floor and basement. On the second floor, there are the commandant's bedchamber, sons' bedchamber, and daughters' bedroom and sitting room. All of the major rooms on both floors have fireplaces. The attic floor contains a cook's bedroom, servants' bedroom, sitting area, and storage space.

OSWEGO CITY HALL

*T*he mid-1800s represented Oswego's most prosperous period as a port, and there was great confidence about the city's future growth and success. A city hall to reflect this economic significance and civic optimism was in order. As with the courthouse, the city selected Horatio Nelson White (1814-1892) to design a monumental edifice. Again, White delivered beyond expectations. He created a magnificent Second Empire style building constructed in 1869-1870 of Onondaga limestone supplied by Randall and Nesdall, a Syracuse stonework firm. It stands four stories tall, including its high basement story that acts as a tall platform on which the rest of the building, with its more ornamented

stonework, sits. There is a dominant central clock tower with elaborate architectural detailing. The impressive French mansard roof is sheathed in bands of polychrome slates. Tall slender arched windows on the third floor add to the vertical emphasis of the structure. White created a final incarnation of the Oswego City Hall Second Empire design when he created the first building for Syracuse University, the Hall of Languages, in 1871-1873. With its huge size and complexity, that university building represents the pinnacle of White's prodigious achievements. By the 1880s, White was in his 70s, and he began a gradual retirement. His obituary in 1892 referred to him as the "venerable architect."

OSWEGO COUNTY COURTHOUSE

Oswego, located on the eastern edge of Lake Ontario, was America's farthest west frontier border during the Revolutionary War. It was the most important battlefront in the War of 1812. Although settlement started in 1800, the real impetus for growth was the completion of the Oswego Canal in 1828, which connected Oswego and Lake Ontario to the Erie Canal and New York State's vast canal system. By 1858, the bustling trading and manufacturing city needed a suitable county courthouse. The prominent Syracuse architect, Horatio Nelson White (1814-1892), was commissioned to design it. In 1856, White had designed the Onondaga County Courthouse in Syracuse, which was such a resounding success that it persuaded Oswego leaders to hire White for their courthouse project. White did not disappoint. By 1860, Oswego had a dramatically impressive courthouse in Renaissance Revival style with a temple-style facade topped by an oversized colonnaded and domed tower. Smaller similar domes supported by columns decorate the roofs of the structure's side wings. Verticality is further emphasized by tall Roman-arched windows on the second floor and slender Corinthian columns between the windows supporting the entablature. The effect of this imposing solid-stone building clearly influenced Oswego's Common Council Building Committee ten years later to hire Horatio Nelson White to design their new city hall as well.

OSWEGO: RICHARDSON-BATES HOUSE

*M*axwell B. Richardson (1838-1903) was a prominent attorney, insurance broker, and two-term mayor of Oswego. His wealth was acquired from buying and selling property, collecting rent from his residential and commercial properties, and investments in mining operations in the west. He inherited a house that his father had built around 1850. But he found it inadequate. Although he was a lifelong bachelor, he aspired to a mansion in which he could live with his widowed mother Naomi Richardson, his divorced sister Harriet Bates, and her son Norman. He commissioned the preeminent Rochester, New York, architect, Andrew Jackson Warner (1833-1910) to design a substantial addition to his existing frame house. Warner created a massive brick Italian Villa style house with a four-story tower, built 1867-1871. Between 1887 and 1889, the original wooden house to the right of the tower was replaced with a brick addition in Italianate style to match Warner's elaborate design. Mr. Richardson's mansion contained 20 rooms, including five bedrooms and six bathrooms. There was a museum room on the third floor of the tower where Richardson showcased his cultural- and natural-history collections. What is particularly amazing about this mansion, which is a house museum today, is that 95 percent of the furnishings are original to the house, and they have been arranged exactly according to photographs of the rooms taken by Norman Bates in 1889. With its opulent furniture and decorative arts of the period, the house presents an authentic glimpse of the Victorian life of wealthy Americans.

Left: Maxwell Richardson's high-ceilinged office remains as he occupied it in the late 1800s.

Top: The living room contains almost all of its original furnishings, which are arranged as they appeared in Victorian times.

Above: The Richardson-Bates House is a massive Italian Villa style mansion.

WATERTOWN: FLOWER MEMORIAL LIBRARY

*T*he Flower Memorial Library was a gift to the city of Watertown from Mrs. Emma Flower Taylor, in memory of her father, Roswell Pettibone Flower (1835-1899), postmaster, jeweler, banker, investment broker, U.S. congressman, and governor of New York State (1892-1894). Emma Flower Taylor laid the cornerstone for the new library on July 11, 1903; the building was completed November 10, 1904. The library design is the work of the architectural firm of Orchard, Lansing & Joralemon, with Addison F. Lansing as the supervisory architect. The classicism of the Beaux Arts style was popular in America at the time, and a subdued version of the style is apparent in the library, constructed of white marble. Emma Flower Taylor had insisted that the library not only represent fine architecture to hold books, but should also be a showplace of excellent art and decoration. To accomplish this requirement, Charles Rollinson Lamb (1860-1942) of New York City was engaged. He was both an artist and an architect, and became famous for his splendid mosaics in the Sage Memorial Chapel at Cornell University and his artistic efforts that improved the beauty of New York City and other major cities in America. Lamb asked the architects to enlarge the rotunda of the library and elevate the dome to more heroic proportions, which resulted in one of the more dramatic public libraries in the U.S. He then filled these spaces of vaulted ceilings with mosaics, painted murals, stained glass, bronze and marble sculptures, oil paintings, gold detailing, and even the signs of the Zodiac in bronze on the central rotunda's beautiful marble floor. If the books do not delight, the library itself certainly will. On Washington Street close to the library is a bronze statue of Governor Roswell P. Flower, created by the famous American sculptor, Augustus St. Gaudens, and erected in 1902.

Left: The domed rotunda of Watertown's Flower Memorial Library is also a sculpture gallery.

Below: One of several reading rooms in the library has a vaulted ceiling and large fireplace.

153

SYRACUSE: NIAGARA MOHAWK BUILDING

*A*rt Deco was the hot architectural style in America during the 1920s and 1930s. The style is characterized by features like smooth wall surfaces (often shiny metal), with zigzags, chevrons, and other geometric motifs as decorative elements on the façade. The geometric motifs usually emphasize verticality, which is often enhanced by adding towers and vertical projections. Even figure sculptures display an angular geometric approach. One of the best examples of Art Deco style in New York State, and arguably in America, is the Niagara Mohawk Building in Syracuse. This dramatic seven-story structure, which is the headquarters of the Niagara Mohawk Power Company at 300 Erie Boulevard West, was built in 1932. It was designed by the Buffalo architectural firm of Bley & Lyman and the Syracuse architect Melvin L. King. The façade is constructed of gray brick and stone in a series of setbacks, with additional cladding in stainless steel, aluminum, and black glass. The ornamentation is truly opulent. There are parallel bands, zigzags, and chevrons. At the base of the tower six stories above the entrance, there is a 28-foot-high statue of a male figure with outstretched arms from which rays of light emanate like giant wings. The stunning sculpture is called, "Spirit of Light." Niagara Mohawk gleams, shimmering in daylight and glittering at night with interior lighting and powerful exterior flood illumination.

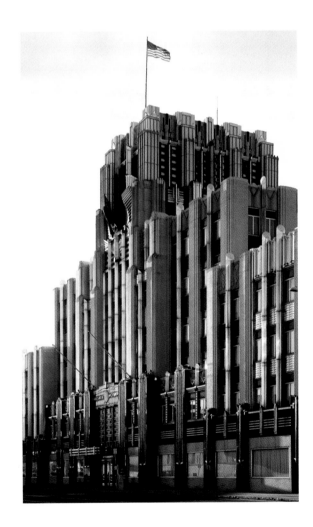

CORTLAND: 1890 HOUSE

At No. 37 Tompkins Street, Cortland's avenue of late 19th-century Gilded Age architecture, stands the grand limestone mansion of Chester Franklin Wickwire. This towered and turreted Chateauesque castle appears to be an absolute original, but it is an exact copy. Chester Wickwire was a farmer near Cortland, who opened a hardware store in the city. Some of his customers could not pay for their purchases in cash and presented barter goods. One customer offered a carpet loom, probably not propitious payment to most storekeepers, but to Chester Wickwire it was the inspiration for a new career. He converted the loom to make screening mesh, like window screens. Then, as ranchers and farmers settled the West, the need for fencing became necessary to separate the two, and Chester devised an inexpensive fencing material: barbed wire. As millions of dollars poured into his vast Cortland factory, he aspired to a new house. Riding a carriage on the streets of New York one day, he selected a house he liked. It was the home of James A. Bailey of Barnum & Bailey Circus, designed by New York City architect Samuel Burrage Reed, whom Wickwire engaged to duplicate that house in Cortland. Construction started in 1888, and 18 months later the Wickwire family moved into their 30-room mansion, a mirror-image of Bailey's eclectic Chateauesque New York City house. The entire house including the towers and turrets is open to the public.

Left: The expansive entrance hall of the 1890 House incorporates an inglenook beneath the grand staircase.

Above Right: One of the 30 rooms in the Wickwire house is the Conservatory with a vaulted glass ceiling.

Right: The parlor reflects the heavily ornate Victorian period.

LETCHWORTH STATE PARK: GLEN IRIS INN

William Pryor Letchworth (1823-1910), at age 25, formed Pratt and Letchworth, which manufactured hardware in Buffalo. He developed a process to make malleable iron that was particularly suited to producing components of harnesses and other saddlery. He longed to live in the country away from city smoke and crowds. One day on a train trip that he took from New York City to Buffalo, the train stopped on a 234-foot-high bridge that overlooked a spectacular gorge with the Genesee River flowing in a series of waterfalls far below. He purchased the land, 190 acres which later grew to over 1,000 acres, and established his Glen Iris Estate, named for the Greek goddess of rainbows. He renovated the existing wood-frame cottage, eventually adding a third story to the structure. He was careful to retain the Greek Revival architecture of the original house in all of the improvements he made. The house overlooked the spectacular 107-foot-high Middle Falls and cliffs 600 feet high. Here, he spent glorious weekends with his friends from Buffalo, his art and book collections, and the surrounding scenic splendor. In 1907, he deeded his estate to New York State with provisions for life use. On December 1, 1910, William Pryor Letchworth died peacefully in his bedroom at Glen Iris. Today, his home, still displaying his furnishings, is an inn and fine restaurant. The estate is now Letchworth State Park, a linear 14,350-acre expanse following the Genesee River for 17 miles of breathtaking scenery commonly called "The Grand Canyon of the East."

Above: View of the gorge from Glen Iris Inn with the 234-foot-high railroad bridge.

KEUKA LAKE, BLUFF POINT: GARRETT MEMORIAL CHAPEL

*T*he Garrett Chapel was built in 1931 as a memorial to Charles Garrett, son of Paul and Evelyn Garrett. Charles died of tuberculosis at the age of 26 years. He was the only surviving son of the Garretts (three other sons died in infancy), who had hoped that Charles would carry on the family name and inherit their several thousand acres of vineyards and a successful winemaking operation. Charles was a graduate of Yale University and married to Marjorie Hodgson. They had no children. The parents, devastated by the early death of their only son, decided to build a memorial chapel to keep his memory alive. It was designed by Mortimer Freehof, a New York City architect, in American Neo-Gothic style with many Norman style details. There is a massive square tower, and door and window openings are round-arched. The two principal spaces are the sanctuary and the crypt, which is located one level below the chapel. Lavish materials were used: random ashlar walls of Pennsylvania granite; roof and terrace of

Vermont slate; chapel floor of Rembrandt slate from Holland; Xanadu onyx from Algeria in the crypt; a crypt reception room with walls of Crab Orchard marble from Tennessee; crypt-entrance double doors of silver bronze with bas-relief panels depicting human activities such as fisher, sower, student, scientist, artisan, sports, music, and painting. There is a veritable museum of stained-glass crypt windows with designs inspired by lines from Tennyson's poems, children's stories like "Wynken, Blynken, and Nod," and Abou ben Adhem. One window depicts the progress of civilization with a Star of Bethlehem, Bill of Rights, printing press, Liberty Bell, and Curtiss airplane (built at Hammondsport within sight of the chapel). The artist who designed the unique stained-glass windows was Frederick Wilson, and the fabricator was Judson Art Glass Studio, both of Los Angeles. The whole is a spectacular place, and the view of Keuka Lake from the high bluff is breathtaking.

FINGER LAKES: SYRACUSE SAVINGS BANK

At age 27 years, the budding young architect, Joseph Lyman Silsbee (1848-1913) designed the Syracuse Savings Bank, 102 North Salina Street, which was built in 1875-1876. It is a monumental High Victorian Gothic sandstone building, an impressive architectural statement to the success that the Erie Canal brought to the city. This huge, majestic landmark in downtown Syracuse was Silsbee's first major commission. Born in Salem, Massachusetts in 1848 and educated at Exeter and Harvard University, he studied architecture at MIT in 1870, the year that its architectural school was founded. It was the first such school in the country. With this splendid education, Silsbee went on to become a prominent architect in America. He moved to Syracuse in 1874, made a great name

for himself there, and in 1882, opened a second office in Buffalo, with huge success there as well. By 1886, he started a third practice in Chicago, where he finally settled. One of his inventions was the moving sidewalk, which he created for the 1893 Chicago Exposition. There are 350 known Silsbee architectural designs throughout America. Silsbee, when he was practicing in Chicago, was the first architect to employ the young Frank Lloyd Wright. In his autobiography, Wright states that Silsbee was one of the greatest influences on Wright's own architectural development. So, Silsbee not only contributed a prodigious number of fine architectural designs to our country, but he significantly influenced the development of our country's greatest architect.

SYRACUSE UNIVERSITY: CROUSE COLLEGE

*A*rchimedes N. Russell (1840-1915), at 6-feet-4-inches and 300 pounds, was a mountain of a man and designed a mountain of buildings, nearly 850 in his 43-year career. Many of those buildings were also mountains in themselves. Consider Crouse College, a monumental four-story Medina sandstone structure with a massive tower, all of which very much dominates Syracuse University's highest knoll. Russell had an agreeable client for this extravagant building: John Crouse, who wanted to build the finest college building in the country, sparing no expense. Crouse, a businessman who was considered the wealthiest person in

Syracuse at the time and was a university trustee, had taken a walk on campus with Chancellor Charles N. Sims and, when they approached the highest hill on campus, Crouse said, "Save this hill for me and I will put a building on it such as you will never regret having here." Crouse College was built between 1887 and 1889. Although there is nothing subtle about the imposing Romanesque Revival structure, it is still graceful and attractive. There is almost an overabundance of decorative details. The elaborate auditorium has complex stained-glass windows that, with the colorful array of Victorian details on the walls, fill the room with bright colors.

CAZENOVIA: LORENZO

*T*he historic village of Cazenovia was founded in 1793 by
John Lincklaen (1768-1822). He emigrated from Holland to
work as the land agent for the Holland Land Company. He laid out
a tract for what he called "a great commercial city in the wilderness." He selected a site on the south end of Cazenovia Lake on
which to build a proper mansion, which he chose to name
"Lorenzo" after Lorenzo di Medici's villa in Florence, which had
neoclassical lines similar to his proposed structure. Having experi-
enced a devastating fire in his first residence, Lincklaen determined
to create a fireproof building by using bricks on both exterior and
interior walls. He installed two-inch thick plaster ceilings and lined
the nine fireplaces with sheet iron. It is believed that John Hooker,
a master builder from Utica designed the gracious, 23-room,
Federal style mansion. Construction began in the spring of 1807,
and the Lincklaen family moved into Lorenzo in the fall of 1808.
Originally, Lorenzo had a red-brick exterior color. It went through
several color schemes before settling on white with brown trim.
Five generations of the family lived here for 160 years before the
New York State Historic Trust took title to the property and
restored the estate, opening it to the public. The Lincklaen family's
collection of historic furnishings is virtually intact.

*The entrance hall, looking toward the
entrance with its Federal style sidelights
and fanlight.*

162

Top: The drawing room of Lorenzo, the 23-room mansion of John Lincklaen.

Above: Lush trees and informal plantings surround a formal flower garden with a central path.

Above left: President Grover Cleveland and New York Governor Horatio Seymour slept in this guest bedroom.

Right: The wide entrance hall of Lorenzo is a synthesis of styles with its bold wallpaper depicting pheasants in brush and tile floor in a geometric pattern. The staircase, with its delicate, slender spindles, however, is original Federal style.

AUBURN: WILLIAM H. SEWARD HOUSE

*T*he man, who in 1867 signed a check for $7,200,000 to purchase Alaska from Russia, was William Henry Seward (1801-1872), U.S. secretary of state in President Lincoln's and President Johnson's cabinets. His historic home at 33 South Street in Auburn, where four generations of the Seward family lived from 1816 to 1951, is a National Historic Landmark. William Seward was governor of New York, U.S. senator, and U.S. secretary of state. His 17-room house, built in 1816-1817, bears elements of both Federal and Tuscan style architecture. It is surrounded by two acres of gardens. This grand house has hosted such distinguished visitors as Elizabeth Cady Stanton, Harriet Tubman, Dorothea Dix, Daniel Webster, Henry Clay, General George A.

Custer, and Presidents John Quincy Adams, Martin Van Buren, Andrew Johnson, Ulysses S. Grant, William McKinley, and Bill Clinton. After he gave an antislavery speech in 1864, Seward became the target of a conspiracy organized by John Wilkes Booth. On April 14, 1865, as he lay in bed recovering from injuries caused by a carriage accident, would-be assassin Lewis Powell stormed into his bedroom and stabbed Seward's throat and heart. Seward rolled around in bed quickly enough to make the knife thrusts through the heavy blankets glancing cuts, and the wire netting supporting his broken jaw protected his throat. Amazingly, Seward recovered. Powell was subsequently arrested, tried, found guilty, and executed.

Top left: The Seward House combines Federal and Tuscan styles with a Victorian interior.

Above left: The parlor displays an enviable collection of original furnishings arranged as they were when the Seward family lived here.

Above: The curving staircase in the front hall has an elaborate Victorian newel post.

Right: The dining room table is set for dinner on original Seward tableware.

GENEVA: ROSE HILL MANSION

*T*he pinnacle of domestic Greek Revival architecture in western New York is Rose Hill Mansion, built in 1838 by William Kerley Strong (1805-1867). When he bought Rose Hill farm in 1837 from the estate of Robert Selden Rose (1774-1835), Strong operated a highly successful wool brokerage business in New York City. He decided to sell it at age 37 years and move to Geneva, taking his fortune and investing a considerable portion of it on a truly grand mansion that stands on an auspicious high point on the 900-acre farm with a splendid view of Seneca Lake. Strong moved Rose's simple farmhouse to the side and converted it to a carriage house, which still stands today. Rose Hill Mansion was completed in 1839, just in time to receive U.S. President Martin Van Buren as one of the first guests. In Geneva, Strong organized and became president of the Farmer's Bank, as well as a trustee of Hobart College. Although Strong may have hired a distinguished architect from New York City to design his house, it is more likely that he employed the creative and highly qualified craftsmen readily available in Geneva. The main pavilion is fronted by a portico that is 51 feet wide with a monumental colonnade of six two-story Ionic columns. These columns are 23 feet high and almost three feet in diameter. The porches on the recessed wings that flank the main block each have two single-story Ionic columns. In the center of the roof is a square Greek Revival cupola. The imposing mansion is of wood construction and painted white, giving it the qualities of a magnificent Greek temple of marble standing on a high hill. Inside, there are spacious rooms, high ceilings with refined plaster work, carved marble fireplace mantels, and Ionic columns separating the front and back parlors. Strong's wife, Sara Ann VanGieson Strong, died, unfortunately, in 1843 at Rose Hill, and Strong left his beloved home to return to New York City. In 1861, President Abraham Lincoln commissioned Strong a Brigadier General, and he served nobly with great patriotism and zeal in the Union Army during the Civil War.

Top: The Music Room contains an American Empire harp in rosewood and gilt. To the left is a three-octave rocking melodeon, and there is a piano, not shown.

Above: Rose Hill Mansion has six bedrooms (five with fireplaces), plus servants' quarters, playroom, sitting room, sewing room, and more.

ITHACA: CORNELL UNIVERSITY, McGRAW HALL

*J*ohn McGraw (1815-1877), partner of Henry W. Sage and also a founding trustee of Cornell University, agreed to finance the construction of McGraw Hall *(right)*. The prolific Syracuse architect, Archimedes N. Russell (1840-1915), was commissioned to design the building, which would contain the university's first library. The building was constructed in 1869-1872 of Cayuga bluestone, which is a richly variegated shale that was formed 355 million years ago, trapping primitive life forms such as corals, brachipods, cystoids, sponges, snails, trilobites, nautiloids, and starfish. The stone in the building is studied regularly by staff and students to identify its fossil content. The bluestone for McGraw Hall was quarried right on the university campus. In fact, many of the first students at Cornell paid for their tuition by excavating the shale in the quarry.

ITHACA: CORNELL UNIVERSITY, SAGE HALL

*I*n 1868, Henry W. Sage (1814-1897), a lumber industrialist and founding trustee of Cornell University, told the school's founder, Ezra Cornell (1807-1874), "When you are ready to carry out the idea of educating young women as thoroughly as young men, I will provide the endowment to enable you to do so." Cornell accepted the offer and Sage Hall *(left)* was built as a combination women's dormitory and classroom building. Construction of the Victorian brick building began in 1872 under the design guidance of the university's professor of architecture, Charles Babcock. With Sage Hall completed in 1875, Cornell University became one of the pioneer coeducational institutions in America. Above the four stories of the façade rises a dramatic spire, and on the rear elevation, a high-peaked tower also pierces the sky, but stops short of the spire's flamboyance.

ITHACA: CORNELL UNIVERSITY, GOLDWIN SMITH HALL

*G*oldwin Smith (1823-1910) left Oxford University in England to become professor of English and constitutional history at Cornell University from its founding in 1868 to 1871. This Greek Revival hall *(above)* with its temple-style portico was named for Goldwin Smith. The statue is of Andrew Dickson White (1832-1918), the first president of Cornell University. White met the school's founder, Ezra Cornell, when they were New York State senators. They had a common vision for this nonsectarian, coeducational school, and White laid the groundwork for Cornell University.

CANANDAIGUA: SONNENBERG MANSION AND GARDENS

*B*ack in 1877, most wealthy New York City residents built their summer homes in Long Island or the Hudson River Valley. Not true for Frederick Ferris Thompson (1836-1899), a prominent New York City banker and founder of the First National Bank of New York City which became Citibank, and his wife Mary Lee Clark Thompson (1835-1923), daughter of New York State governor, Myron Holley Clark. Thompson met his future wife in Albany at the governor's mansion when he was doing financial business there. They were married in 1857. Mary Clark and her family, who were from beautiful Canandaigua, suggested they build a summer house there. In 1863, they purchased 52 acres at 151 Charlotte Street and built the mansion in 1885-1887 on the highest ground at the estate, calling it Sonnenberg, which is German for "sunny hill." Although the Thompsons owned a townhouse at 283 Madison Avenue in New York City, a cottage in Maine, and a 20,000-acre estate in the Carolinas, Sonnenberg was their favorite home. Their three-story, 40-room Victorian house is constructed of rusticated gray stone, trimmed in Medina sandstone, and gables of half timber and stucco. The roof is slate and lead-coated copper. The style is Queen Anne, which borrowed details from various architectural styles, in this case, a blend of Elizabethan, Tudor, and Romanesque. The architect was Francis R. Allen (1844-1931) of Boston, who seems to have been strongly influenced by the works of one of America's greatest architects, Henry Hobson Richardson (1838-1886), who invented Richardsonian Romanesque style. The major rooms on the first floor are the two-story Great Hall, grand dining room, trophy room, billiard room, library, and circular rotunda. There are a number of other buildings on the estate, including the domed Palm House, which is the centerpiece of the conservatory complex and contains 1,100 pieces of curved, frosted glass. Ernest W. Bowdich, a leading landscape architect from Boston, designed the nine gardens between 1902 and 1919.

Above: The balcony with a beamed ceiling is above the Great Hall at Sonnenberg.

Right: A Greek Revival style pavilion is the architectural focal point in the rose garden.

Middle right: The porch off the circular rotunda overlooks the fabulous gardens.

Far right: A dramatic architectural feature in the Japanese garden is the oriental pagoda.

CANANDAIGUA: GRANGER HOMESTEAD

Gideon Granger, Jr. (1767-1822) was a native of Connecticut and was graduated from Yale University in 1787, after which he practiced law until age 25, when he was elected a Connecticut state legislator, serving for nine years until 1801. Granger worked hard to get Thomas Jefferson elected U.S. president, who rewarded Granger by appointing him postmaster general in 1801. Granger, in turn, appointed Seth Pease first assistant postmaster general. Pease was the brother of Granger's wife, Mindwell Pease, whom he had married in 1790. Granger continued as U.S. postmaster general into President James Madison's term before retiring in 1814 and moving his family to Canandaigua, New York, thereby locating himself closer to his land tracts further to the west. On 10 acres of scenic property at 295 North Main Street just a few blocks from downtown Canandaigua, Granger built a homestead that he said would be "unrivaled in all the nation." The magnificent Federal style mansion, inspired by the works of the distinguished British architect, Robert Adam, took two years to build and was completed in 1816. Typical features of the style are the slender paired columns supporting the entrance portico of the Granger house and the central placement of the entrance with symmetrically positioned windows on either side of the entrance. On the second and third floors, each bay is distinguished by slender pilasters. The first and second floors contain five bays which are reduced to three bays on the third floor. Handsome balustrades line the second- and third-floor roofs. Four generations of the Granger family occupied the house, which is now a museum incorporating the original elaborately hand-crafted moldings and fireplace mantels, as well as much of the original furnishings. There are historic carriage barns that house a collection of more than 50 19th-century horse-drawn vehicles.

Opposite page: Elegant Federal style motifs are carved into the door, window, and fireplace wood-frame elements in the north parlor.

Top left: The sleigh bed in a second-floor bedroom is embellished by a draped corona. A writing desk is in the foreground.

Middle left: The dining room features a reprint of a historic wallpaper border below the crown molding.

Left: An 1822 Greek Revival law office was moved to the Granger site to replace the original similar structure that stood on this site. Lawyers in the 1800s typically worked in small buildings like this.

ROCHESTER: GEORGE EASTMAN HOUSE

George Eastman (1854-1932)—founder of the great photographic enterprise, Eastman Kodak Company—built his dream house at 900 East Avenue in 1905. It is a 35,000-square-foot mansion in Georgian Revival style with 37 rooms, 13 baths, and 9 fireplaces. The baronial edifice is the largest single-family house in Monroe County and is as close to what the English call a "stately home" as it gets in these parts. Inspired by the Columbian Exposition at Chicago in 1893, architecture in America returned to more classical models during the first decade of the 20th century, and the preeminent creator of classical architecture in America at the time was the prestigious firm of McKim, Mead & White in New York City. They—in association with the prominent Rochester architect, John Foster Warner—designed Eastman's vast house in which he lived as a bachelor, although he entertained regularly. Eastman had at his disposal a huge music room/conservatory with a giant Aeolian pipe organ, an elegant dining room with a beautiful silver chandelier, a billiard room with a raised platform from which guests could watch games, a cozy library for intimate conversations, a sprawling living room where musical ensembles delivered concerts, a spacious entrance hall with a grand staircase, and other rooms, all on the first floor. Guests would arrive at the porte cochere on the west side of the mansion, and the women would be whisked upstairs to shed their coats and check their makeup before descending the grand staircase to meet their escorts awaiting in the entrance hall. It was an impressive scene, reminiscent of 19th-century European balls. When Eastman moved in, he noted that the conservatory seemed too square and that the proportions should be made more rectangular, so he ordered that the house be cut in half and the rear part moved back nine feet. The effort cost more than the original house itself, and his architect, J. Foster Warner, noted, "I learned a lesson in proportions." Today, the meticulously restored house is a National Historic Landmark.

Above: Lavish gardens surround the
Eastman House; here is the Rock Garden
on the north side of the estate.

Left: The Eastman House grand staircase was designed by William Rutherford Mead of McKim, Mead & White, New York City.

Above: The Eastman House Terrace Garden has two antique Italian well-heads as focal points.

Right: George Eastman breakfasted in the conservatory while his private organist played favorite selections on the giant Aeolian pipe organ. The pipes are hidden behind the second floor hall.

181

ROCHESTER CITY HALL

*I*n 1882, the U.S. Congress authorized $300,000 to build a federal building in Rochester. The supervising architect in the Treasury Department was 36-year-old Mifflin Bell, and critics maintain that this Richardsonian Romanesque building was his best work. Others attribute the design to Rochester artist and architect, Harvey Ellis. In any case, by 1886, the masonry work was completed to the second story. Then, the government, in its infinite wisdom, decided to authorize an additional $200,000 for a bigger building, so the plans had to be redesigned and a larger building started. The massive building—with its thick walls, high towers, and arched windows all in Medina sandstone—was built between 1885 and 1889. Italian

masons carved the numerous stone adornments including a winged eagle and a medieval dragon on the exterior. In the 1970s, the federal government abandoned the building altogether to erect a still larger structure at another location. So the city of Rochester, which also needed more space, took ownership of the old federal building, renovated it, and added a 45,000-square-foot addition to make it Rochester's current City Hall. The spectacular atrium is breathtaking with its lavish carved stone arches supported by columns of Tennessee marble and elaborately carved capitals. Between the arches are sculpted heads of goddesses, lions, and Neptune. It is a dramatic setting for frequent public events.

ROCHESTER: MONROE COUNTY OFFICE BUILDING

*T*he Monroe County Office Building in Rochester was formerly the county courthouse, the third courthouse built on this site. This elegant building was designed by local architect J. Foster Warner in Italian Renaissance Revival style—the first example of this style built in western New York. It was constructed between 1894 and 1896. The opulent interior of the building has a center atrium with Italian marble walls. Four different styles of columns support the arched hallways around the atrium on the four above-ground floors. Several types of Italian marble cover the floors, stairs, door frames, and columns. Interior office and meeting-room walls are clad in Cuban mahogany, and there are intricate designs in brass, copper, and iron. The hallway and elaborate frieze shown here are on the top floor of this luxurious structure.

MUMFORD: GENESEE COUNTRY VILLAGE AND MUSEUM

*I*n 1966, John (Jack) L. Whele, Rochester industrialist and lifelong collector of sporting art (in fact, it is North America's premier collection of wildlife and sporting art), bought several hundred acres of land in a wild state on a rise above Oatka Creek near the village of Mumford with the intention of creating a village of 19th-century buildings. The buildings would not be reproductions; they would be actual, existing structures that represented a cross section of 19th-century life. Wehle scoured the countryside for suitable architectural examples and moved them to Mumford. He bought the Octagon House, circa 1870, and moved it from Friendship in Allegany County to the museum grounds. He acquired the Greek Revival birthplace of George Eastman, who was born in Waterville, New York. He obtained a pioneer log cabin, several historic churches, a steepled town hall, a blacksmith shop, elaborate

Victorian houses like the Second Empire Hamilton Mansion, the Greek Revival Livingston-Backus House, carriage houses, commercial buildings, farm buildings—altogether 59 structures that created a true Genesee Country village. Each structure was meticulously restored and furnished with appropriate period furniture and decorative arts. The mansions were surrounded by carefully tended formal gardens. Live demonstrations by "villagers" in period dress include blacksmithing, cooking, spinning, gardening, printing, merchandising, and more. Finally, there is Whele's world-class art collection of sporting art from France, England, and America. The collection also includes wildlife artists like Audubon and Tunnicliffe and a trotting horse gallery filled with oil paintings, sculptures, and lithographs recalling American trotting scenes. The living history museum is the largest in New York State, and third largest in the U.S.

Counterclockwise from top left: The Hamilton Second Empire Mansion and carriage house, the Jones farmhouse, the church behind a historic wooden fence, and the Octagon House.

ROCHESTER: MEMORIAL ART GALLERY

*J*ohn Gade, a prominent New York City architect, designed the main building of the Memorial Art Gallery in 1913. The inspiration for the neoclassical style structure was the Malatesta Temple in Rimini, Italy. The gallery was a gift to the University of Rochester from Emily Sibley Watson in memory of her son from her first marriage, James G. Averell, a young architect who died of typhoid at age 26 years. Just a few months before his death in 1904, Averell sketched the Malatesta Temple, so his mother requested that architect John Gade, her nephew-in-law, design the new art gallery building after her son's favorite temple. The great Fountain Court inside the building features a 22-foot-high Italian Baroque pipe organ with an ornately carved, painted and gilded case topped by an unusual St. Andrew crown motif. The organ dates to circa 1770 and contains 600 pipes, most of which are even earlier, probably circa 1700. It is the only full-sized antique Italian pipe organ in North America. Its majestic sound can be heard at regular organ concerts.

Left: The Herdle Fountain Court in the Memorial Art Gallery houses a 22-foot-high Baroque pipe organ.

Top: The 1913 gallery building was modeled after the Malatesta Temple in Italy.

Above: A 1987 addition tied the gallery to the Cutler Union, a grand Collegiate Gothic building, built in 1932-1933.

Right: An entrance detail of Cutler Union, which now contains art gallery offices, library, auditorium, meeting rooms, and a restaurant.

ROCHESTER: SUSAN B. ANTHONY HOUSE

Susan Brownell Anthony (1820-1906) started teaching school at age 15 years, but after age 30, she became a pioneer crusader, devoting her life to furthering women's rights. She and Elizabeth Cady Stanton founded the National Woman Suffrage Association in 1869, and Anthony became its president. In the presidential election of 1872, she led a group of women to a polling booth in Rochester and demanded to vote. As the ringleader, she was arrested, tried, convicted, and fined $100. But she persisted. She wrote, "The right of citizens of the United States to vote shall not be denied or abridged by the United States or by any State on account of sex." These 28 words, known as the Anthony Amendment, became law as the 19th Amendment to the U.S. Constitution in 1920, 14 years after her death. After her father died in 1862, Susan's mother bought, in 1866, a two-story, red-brick Victorian vernacular house at 17 Madison Street, in a middle-class neighborhood. A third floor was added in the 1890s. Neither Susan B. nor her sister, Mary, were married, and they shared the house until their deaths. At Mary's 70th birthday, Susan B. said, "I cannot tell how she has helped and sustained me. She has kept a home where I might come to rest. From the very beginning, she has cheered and comforted me. She has looked after the great mass of details, my wardrobe, my business, leaving me free. Without Mary my work would have been impossible." Today, the modest house sits in a neighborhood of 19th-century Victorian houses that surround a public square containing, besides lawn and mature trees, life-size bronze statues of Susan B. Anthony and her friend and associate, Frederick Douglass, seated having tea and conversation. Inside the National Historic Landmark house, hundreds of objects tell the history of the time when Susan B. worked so hard to change women's lives for the better.

Above: With its decorative spinning wheel and collection of books, this study on the third floor was where Susan B. Anthony composed her many writings.

Top: The Anthony house is a modest Victorian red-brick, three-story residence in Rochester's Susan B. Anthony Preservation District.

Above: The front parlor was where U.S. marshal Elisha J. Keeney arrested Anthony after she voted illegally in the presidential election of 1872.

PITTSFORD, BUSHNELL'S BASIN: RICHARDSON'S CANAL HOUSE

*J*ust west of Bushnell's Basin, Irondequoit Creek flows through the deep, wide Irondequoit Valley which presented one of the greatest challenges to the construction of the Erie Canal. From rim to rim, the valley extended one mile. Running through the valley, however, were three natural ridges, and the solution lay in connecting them with gigantic earth-and-stone embankments, one of which was 1,320 feet long. The resulting canal skyway extends for a mile 40 to 76 feet above the valley floor, and the creek flows through a huge stone culvert. In 1818, the stupendous four-year task was begun with picks, shovels, and wheelbarrows. Also in 1818, a 2 1/2-story, Federal style inn/tavern was constructed at Bushnell's Basin—a particularly insightful decision considering all the canal workers and traveling canal supervisors who might need food, drink, and lodging. It is still a restaurant today (much more upscale than in 1818, of course) called Richardson's Canal House, 1474 Marsh Road. The Erie Canal flows within a few feet of its front entrance. It is the oldest original Erie Canal inn still in its original form and still on the canal. The building boasts its original exterior and interior architectural details, including its distinctive initial exterior color, a bright yellow ochre. The Federal style was popular from the Revolutionary War to the 1830s, and some of the Federal touches at Richardson's include a low-pitched roof, tall chimneys, symmetrical placement of windows on either side of the center entrance, pillared two-story porches on the façade, narrow sidelights at the entrance doorway, and multi-paned windows. If those early canal workers on the Great Embankment had the energy left at the end of a work day, they could bounce around on the spring dance floor on the second floor.

Above: The library with the north front parlor beyond the arched, elaborately carved wood partition. The painting above the fireplace is of St. Sebastian.

Right: A stained-glass window detail in the dining room.

Middle: There are large double parlors on the south side of the house.

Far right: The dining room has a bay of windows with diamond-shaped panes.

BROCKPORT: MORGAN-MANNING HOUSE

Dayton Samuel Morgan joined William H. Seymour to form Seymour & Morgan Iron Works in 1846. It was the first manufactory in America to mass produce farm machinery when they undertook a contract from Cyrus McCormick, inventor of the first machine to harvest wheat, to produce his reaper. Before then, reapers were built one-at-a-time by blacksmiths. When McCormick's patents expired, Seymour & Morgan designed and manufactured reapers on their own. Production increased to as many as 3,000 harvesters a year, and the firm had branch offices across the U.S. and exported them to Europe as well. When Seymour retired in 1877, Morgan purchased his patents and continued the firm, calling it D. S. Morgan & Company, and operated it until his death in 1892. When he became a wealthy man, Morgan acquired an impressive house at 151 Main Street, which had been built in 1856. It is a large Italianate red-brick structure with a full-width porch on the façade supported by eight fluted and belted wood columns. Inside, there are double parlors on either side of a central hall. Featured at left are the handsomely restored double rooms on the north side of the house. In the foreground is the library and behind an arched partial wall is the reception parlor. Elaborately carved wood with classical motifs covers the walls, ceilings, and fireplace surrounds. Pairs of square, fluted wood columns with Ionic capitals support the wooden arches separating the two rooms. The heavy crown moldings are made of carved wood instead of plaster and incorporate a dentil motif. Completing the Victorian look are brass chandeliers, their only exception to authenticity being wired for electricity. For 100 years, the large house was the home of Dayton Morgan and later generations of his family. When Morgan, Brockport's leading citizen, died in April 1892, his funeral was held in this house. Nearly 500 people packed the interior for the funeral, and more than that number stood on the porch and grounds. The *Rochester Herald* estimated that nearly 2,000 mourners attended.

CHILDS: COBBLESTONE CHURCH

Cobblestone architecture is unique to the United States and 90 percent of it can be found within a 60-mile radius of Rochester. It was a western New York construction technique of building sturdy structures from rubble stone faced with small rounded stones laid in horizontal rows and held in place by lime-based mortar. When the Erie Canal was completed in 1825, canal masons (mostly immigrants from Europe) needed work. They noticed that farmers, in clearing their fields, collected piles of rounded stones just sitting in unused mounds. The smooth stones were created by glacier and lake movement, and when the glaciers retreated 14,000 years ago and Lake Ontario's shoreline receded by several miles, the stones were left spotting the fields that farmers wanted to till. The unemployed masons offered their services to construct buildings that could be decorated with stones sorted by desired shape, color, and size. To be classified as a cobblestone, the stone must fit in a person's hand. The Cobblestone Church on Route 104 in Childs was built in 1834 of stones gathered from surrounding fields and carted to the site by oxen. There are 26 cobblestone churches in western New York and this one is the oldest. The corner quoins are rough-cut limestone. The 20-over-20 double-hung windows attest to a time when glass could not be fashioned in large dimensions thereby requiring all those muntins to contain the small panes. The cobblestones were usually laid with the long sides into the wall and the small ends exposed. The general practice was to use the smaller stones on the façade and the larger ones on the side and back walls of a structure. The stone inscription over the front door of this church states: "Erected by the First Universalist Society A.D. 1834." During and 1840s and 1850s, George M. Pullman, inventor of the Pullman railroad car, was a member of this church before he moved to Chicago. Today, the Cobblestone Society owns the church and operates it as a museum and cobblestone resource center. It is a National Historic Landmark.

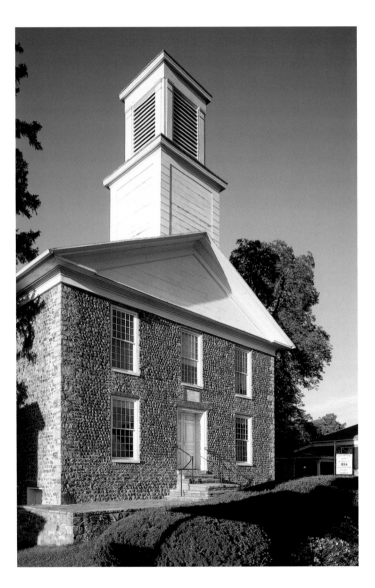

Left: The Cobblestone Society Museum also includes a former town hall built in 1855; behind it are a historic harness shop, print shop, and blacksmith shop.

Above: The 1834 cobblestone church in Childs is the oldest such church in New York State.

Right: The cobblestone church was built from fieldstones; the corner quoins are limestone. To be a cobblestone, it must fit in a person's hand.

CHAUTAUQUA INSTITUTION: ATHENAEUM HOTEL

*T*he sprawling Athenaeum Hotel faces a broad lawn that slopes down past great old trees to the shore of picturesque Lake Chautauqua. It is a splendid view from the rocking chairs on the wide porch of the hotel. The central portion of the porch is two stories high and its roof is supported by tall slender columns. Flanking porches have levels on the first and second floors. With its central mansard-roofed tower, the structure qualifies as Second Empire style. The hotel was built in 1881 and is one of many public buildings in the village, including a 5,000-seat amphitheater built in 1893, churches, schools, sports facilities, art galleries, theaters, library, bell tower, restaurants, shops, and more. The 750-acre Victorian village was designated a National Historic Landmark in 1989 and, in toto, is quite a remarkable architectural phenomenon.

CHAUTAUQUA INSTITUTION: LEWIS MILLER COTTAGE

*L*ewis Miller was a businessman, an inventor, and an educator. As part of his farm-implement business, he invented a mower and plow. As an educator, he co-founded, with Methodist Bishop John Heyl Vincent, the Chautauqua Assembly in 1874. Their religious meetings by Chautauqua Lake originally lasted two weeks in the summer. But they soon expanded to include secular subjects and became nondenominational. Today, the Chautauqua Institution offers programs in art, music, politics, religion, education, and science through the entire summer and even into the fall. In addition, there are symphony concerts, lectures, art exhibits, opera, theater, ballet, and recreation. A third of a million visitors pass through the entrance gates each summer. In 1875, Miller built a two-story frame Victorian cottage, which became his residence. Most of the other several hundred residences in the village are also in Victorian Gothic style.

Above: A Greek Revival temple-style church, Hall of Christ, at Chautauqua Institution.

Below: The Hultquist Center is a building devoted to special studies.

Right: A private home with an elaborate two-story porch.

Opposite: A classical arch announces the entrance to a Greek Revival style open-air auditorium, the Hall of Philosophy.

Left: A second-floor front bedroom has a door to a small balcony over the entrance portico. A Federal style fanlight over the door adds light to the room.

Near right: The front parlor of the McClurg house.

Far right: The library features an ornate secretary and a high writing table.

WESTFIELD: JAMES McCLURG HOUSE

James McClurg was a Scottish emigrant from Ireland, arriving in America with his parents and siblings in 1798. They settled in Pittsburgh and established the first iron foundry there. It was hugely successful, but the adventurous James McClurg, when he became an adult, wanted to strike out on his own rather than join the manufacturing firm. In 1809, his father gave him several thousand dollars, a fortune then, to start his own career somewhere in the wilderness. He chose a tiny log-cabin settlement, purchased land that largely encompassed current Westfield, married the daughter of a nearby settler, and began to build a house. It was 1818; there were no architects in the wilderness; and the current favorite architectural style in America was Federal, adapted primarily from the work of English architect Robert Adam. So, with sketchy knowledge of what a proper house should be in a place where the existing examples were log cabins, McClurg jogged his memory of Pittsburgh houses and may have consulted a pattern book before constructing a highly personal adaptation of the Federal style. Some of those Federal features include symmetry of the façade, semi-elliptical fanlights over the entrance door and second-floor balcony entrance, and recessed arches around the windows. Other distinctive features are the stepped brick gables, the decorative chimneys, cornice molding, and stepped-back wings that flank the central portion of the house. The side porch, single-story shed-roofed addition, and entrance porch with metal columns are all conspicuous later changes. McClurg made his own bricks, fired his own lime for plaster, prepared interior wood from timber on his own land, but he hired skilled bricklayers and carpenters from his native Pittsburgh to build this fine home.

ELMIRA: CHEMUNG COUNTY COURTHOUSE

The Chemung County Courthouse complex comprises four buildings—courthouse (1861), county clerk's office (1875) and annex (1895), and district attorney's and treasurer's building (1836). Shown are the Romanesque Revival courthouse and, to the left, the Greek Revival district attorney's and treasurer's building with a Classical Revival portico designed by Pierce & Bickford Architects and added in 1899. The courthouse was designed by Horatio Nelson White (1814-1892), a prominent Syracuse architect. Roman arches dominate the façade of the courthouse; three arches form the entrance; there are tall narrow arched windows above the first floor including a grand Palladian triple window; four arched fenestrations in the square tower, and arched castellations above the cornices. The Roman and Greek structures stand compatibly side by side. Horatio White started as a carpenter/builder in Andover, Massachusetts, moved to Syracuse in 1843, and became well known as a building contractor. In 1849, he worked in San Francisco in the building boom during the Gold Rush, but returned to Syracuse in the early 1850s to become a highly successful New York State architect. His design for the celebrated Onondaga County Courthouse in Syracuse was the style inspiration for the Chemung County Courthouse.

ELMIRA: THE MARK TWAIN STUDY

One of the most famous literary landmarks in America is the Mark Twain Study. It is a Victorian octagonal structure with windows on all eight sides and resembles the pilot house of a 19th-century Mississippi steamboat, which is precisely what Susan Langdon Crane, the sister of Twain's wife, requested (Twain was a Mississippi River steamboat pilot at age 16) when she commissioned the design of a freestanding study from architect Alfred H. Thorp as a gift to Twain in 1874. Samuel Clemens (a.k.a. Mark Twain) (1835-1910) married Olivia Langdon in 1870, and although the couple lived in Hartford, Connecticut during winter months, they spent summers in Elmira on Quarry Farm with their in-laws, Susan and Theodore Crane. Olivia didn't like all the cigar smoke that Sam created when he was writing in the main house, so Susan came up with the Mark Twain Study solution. Twain loved the gift; he spent 20 summers writing in that study. In 1886, he wrote: "The three months that I spend here are usually my working months. I am free here and can work uninterruptedly, but in Hartford I don't try to do any literary work. Yes, this may be called the home of *Huckleberry Finn* and other books of mine for they were written here." Other books written in the study include *The Adventures of Tom Sawyer, A Tramp Abroad, Life on the Mississippi, The Prince and the Pauper, A Connecticut Yankee in King Arthur's Court,* and more. The Mark Twain Library is also housed at Elmira College, and the study was moved to the campus in 1952. Quarry Farm is also the property of Elmira College, and Mark Twain is buried in Elmira's Woodlawn National Cemetery. During the Civil War, 12,000 Confederate prisoners were incarcerated in Elmira, and many of them died and were interred in Woodlawn, the only cemetery north of the Mason-Dixon line where Confederate soldiers are buried.

ALFRED: CELADON TILE COMPANY OFFICE

*I*n 1889, the Celadon Terra Cotta Company was founded to manufacture bricks and roofing tile from shale mined in local glacial cuts. The shale produced a high-quality clay that was first used to make bricks that possessed a greenish glaze resembling the color celadon of ancient Chinese ceramic ware—hence the company name. The Celadon Company also made ornamental tiles to decorate the exteriors of houses and commercial buildings. When the company constructed an office on Main Street in the village of Alfred, they took examples of their distinctive tiles and incorporated them into the exterior walls of the building, thereby allowing customers to view the whole product line in an outdoor display. It was such an unusual building that the company constructed a replica of it for the 1893 Columbian Exposition in Chicago. As the company grew, it established a school in Alfred for the study of clay-making, which eventually became the College of Ceramics at the State University of New York at Alfred. Fire destroyed the large factory in 1909, but the little office was spared. The Celadon Company's decorative tiles included bas-relief heads, fruit, and geometric designs—all shown here on the four walls of the office beneath a Celadon Company tile roof.

BINGHAMTON: BROOME COUNTY COURTHOUSE

*T*he Broome County Courthouse in Binghamton was designed by hometown architect, Isaac G. Perry (1822-1904), the architect who, in 1883, was appointed to finish the new state capitol in Albany. The courthouse was efficiently built in 1897-1898, while the New York State Capitol, started in 1867, remained under construction until 1899. The courthouse, which sits on a large square in the center of Binghamton, is a massive neoclassical stone structure that seems more imposing than is necessary for a county courthouse. The frieze of the portico is punctuated with a row of round windows that extend across the façade. Six two-story, fluted Ionic columns support the impressive portico, above which rises a Baroque style dome that sits atop a tall octagonal drum. Four clock faces in elaborate Baroque copper frames present the time of day in four directions. High above the ground, above a cupola that tops the dome, stands a statue of Justice with her outstretched left arm displaying a balanced scale. It all borders on the excessive, but is quite an architectural monument to behold. Isaac Perry was a nationally recognized prolific architect, mostly of large buildings like banks, churches, municipal buildings, mansions, hospitals, high schools, and 19 armories, many of which are listed in the National Register of Historic Places.

JOHNSON CITY: SACRED HEART UKRAINIAN CATHOLIC CHURCH

*H*igh on a hill—overlooking the Triple Cities of Binghamton, Johnson City, and Endicott—is Sacred Heart Ukrainian Catholic Church, constructed in 1977 completely of wood with all of its elements copied from existing 17th- and 18th-century churches that themselves follow centuries-earlier design traditions in the Carpathian Mountains of eastern Europe. The church was designed by the noted Ukrainian architect, Apollinare Osadca (1916-1997), who studied architecture at Lviv Polytechnical Institute and worked as an architect in Lviv, Ukraine, before emigrating in 1950 to practice architecture in New York City. The Johnson City church consists of three adjoining squares (entrance hall or narthex, nave, and altar or apse) fronted by a decorative wooden porch. Each of these three elements is surmounted by a dramatic double-onion dome. The exterior is distinguished by traditional Carpathian skirt roofs. Inside, the central dome is open to create a dramatic height in the small nave. There is a choir gallery supported by laminated-wood arches and a huge carved-wood chandelier with symbolic designs. And there are painted wall icons of Byzantine and Russian saints, a pierced-wood icon screen, and other painted decorative elements. The Triple Cities has 18 magnificent Eastern Catholic and Orthodox domed churches, reflecting the many immigrants from Ukraine, Lithuania, Poland, Greece, Armenia, and Slovakia, who came to the area to work in the shoe and cigar factories.

Right: The sanctuary is filled with painted wall icons and a huge carved-wood chandelier.

BUFFALO: CITY HALL

With the stock market crash in October 1929, America entered the Great Depression, which hit Buffalo particularly hard. Yet from 1929 to 1931, one of the most lavish and monumental buildings in Buffalo was erected—the 32-story, 566,313-square-foot City Hall at 65 Niagara Square. Its extravagant decorative details and enormous size are totally contrary to the economic austerity of the period. Today, Buffalo City Hall is regarded as one of the finest Art Deco public buildings in America. It is a credit to the city of Buffalo that it was accomplished in the worst years of the Depression. Despite its massive size, the building displays a graceful, towering presence. At any moment, you expect Superman to swoop from its stylish and futuristic façade. The designer for this great architectural achievement is New York City architect, John J. Wade, who was not shy about creating a building to express a brighter and noble future for Buffalo. He said that the structure "expresses primarily the masculinity, power, and purposeful energy of a great industrial community." The building of gray granite, limestone, and warm sandstone is handsomely adorned with glazed ceramic tiles that add brilliant color to the drum of the tower's glass dome. Other decoration celebrates Buffalo's position as the Queen City of the Lakes. In the carved frieze above the eight giant columns of the main entrance, there are 21 figures tracing Buffalo's preeminence in transportation, lake shipping, steel, petrochemicals, electricity production, architecture, education, and quality of life for its citizens. The great bronze doors of the entrance display symbols of the Indian tribes that once ruled this area. Inside, the lobby reflects the city's energy and vitality with marble floors, mosaic ceilings, and picturesque murals. The Common Council chamber on the 13th floor is illuminated by an enormous semicircular sunburst skylight.

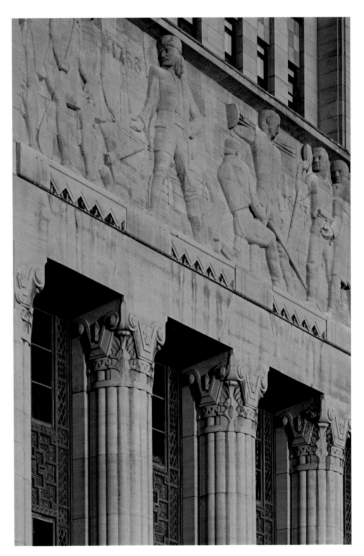

Above: The Common Council chamber on the 13th floor of Buffalo City Hall is illuminated by an enormous semicircular sunburst skylight.

Right: A carved-stone frieze traces Buffalo's preeminence in transportation, lake shipping, steel, petrochemicals, electricity production, architecture, education, and quality of life.

BUFFALO: DARWIN D. MARTIN HOUSE

*D*arwin D. Martin (1865-1935) was secretary of the Larkin Company in Buffalo. He started to work for the company at age 14 and became an exuberant sales representative and accounting genius for the mail-order soap and housewares firm. During Christmas 1900, Martin visited his brother William E. Martin in Oak Park, Illinois, where he was shown houses designed by the young architect, Frank Lloyd Wright. Darwin Martin was instantly impressed with Wright's work and commissioned him to design a house for the Martin family at 125 Jewett Parkway. The house was under construction from 1904 to 1906, and Martin complained frequently about delays in furnishing completed blueprints, causing Wright to respond, "Drawings are not going to leave this office for your buildings until they are right and fit to use as nearly so as we can make them at least, even if you wander homeless for the rest of your mortal days." When complaints continued, Wright wrote: "D.D.M. shall have the most perfect thing of its kind in the world—a domestic symphony, true, vital, and comfortable. A real something to show for his years of hard work, and a translation of those hard, faithful years into a permanent record that will proclaim him to subsequent generations as a lover of the good! the true! the beautiful! For did he not consider the lilies of the field? 'For I say unto thee that Solomon in all his glory was not arrayed like one of these.' Was his home not as a lily of the field? The field? The human soul. There now—will you be good?" Critics place the house in the top 10 most important residential works of Frank Lloyd Wright. Dr. Frank Kowsky, New York State Preservation Board, wrote: "The Martin house is the most important piece of domestic architecture in New York State." Wright was 35 years old when he designed the house, one of the largest and most complex of his Prairie style buildings. It has an open plan allowing a free flow of space between rooms and from the interior to the exterior. In the 10,000-square-foot house, there is a 70-foot-long room that serves as library, living, and dining areas. Because he was given an unlimited budget, Wright designed the furniture, including the first version of his famous barrel chair. In 1986, the house was designated a National Historic Landmark.

Oppossite page: The windows in the Darwin Martin House were designed by Frank Lloyd Wright.

Far left: The Gardener's Cottage is part of the Darwin Martin estate. The gardener of this wood-and-stucco cottage was Reuben Polder, who had to provide fresh flowers daily for every room in the main house, a task that he assiduously accomplished until his employer died in 1935.

Left: The dining room of the Gardener's Cottage—palatial for a gardener.

Above: In 1927, Frank Lloyd Wright designed a stone-and-stucco summer house for the Darwin Martin family on Lake Erie.

Right: The first of Frank Lloyd Wright's Buffalo buildings was the brick George Barton House (1903-1904), built by Darwin Martin for his sister and brother-in-law.

Oppsite page: In 1929, Frank Lloyd Wright completed the design for a mausoleum for Darwin Martin, but after the stock market crash, he couldn't afford it. With grants, Forest Lawn Cemetery in Buffalo built the "Blue Sky Mausoleum," so named by Wright, in 2004.

BUFFALO: FOREST LAWN CEMETERY, FRANK LLOYD WRIGHT'S BLUE SKY MAUSOLEUM

*S*eventy-six years ago, America's great architect, Frank Lloyd Wright (1867-1959), designed a mausoleum for the Darwin D. Martin family. Martin was secretary of the Larkin Company, a large mail-order soap and housewares firm in Buffalo. Then in October 1929, the stock market crashed and Martin lost the means to pay for it. In 2004, Forest Lawn Cemetery on Delaware Avenue accumulated grants of more than half-a-million dollars to construct Wright's mausoleum design, the only one he ever created. When Wright submitted his plan in 1928, he wrote to Martin, "This is a burial facing the open sky, a dignified great headstone common to all. There is a nice symbolism in the stepping terraces, it seems. The scheme is a compromise between the grave and the mausoleum; it may have the better points of both. Executed in good materials, the inscriptions either well carved or inlaid in bronze. The whole could not fail of noble effect." Rather than a traditional mausoleum, it was a series of shallow steps with a center walk. On either side of each step, there was a stone-covered, inground vault for full-body casket burials. It was an idea unique to cemeteries in 1928. Looking at the design with the vaults open to the sky, instead of with a roof over them, Martin dubbed the memorial, "The Martin Blue Sky Mausoleum"—first in recognition that it was open to the sky and also that it would probably cost a fortune. The white granite mausoleum is 50 feet long, over 21 feet wide, and accommodates 48 full-body burials in its 24 double-tiered vaults. It is located in Section 15 between Jubilee Springs and Crystal Lake.

BUFFALO: ALBRIGHT-KNOX ART GALLERY

*I*n 1900, Guilford Smith, president of the Buffalo Fine Arts
Academy, received the greatest letter of his lifetime. It was
from John Joseph Albright (1848-1931), the financier, industrialist,
and entrepreneur who formed Lackawanna Steel Company, later
Bethlehem Steel. It read: "As a lover of art and a believer in its
beneficent influence in such a city as ours, I have long felt that the
academy could not fulfill the purposes of its founders and friends
without the possession of a permanent and suitable home. Such a
home should be exclusively devoted to art, and in its architecture
and surroundings should of itself represent the nature of its
occupancy. From such inquiries as I have been able to make, I am
led to believe that a suitable building would cost from $300,000
to $350,000. This expenditure I am ready to meet." The building
that Albright bought eventually cost him over $1 million, but it is
a masterpiece of elegant architecture. Edward Brodhead Green
(1855-1950), arguably Buffalo's greatest and most prolific architect,
designed it in Neoclassical style. Eighteen marble columns stretch
across the façade of the Albright-Knox Art Gallery, and eight
marble classical caryatids support the flanking porches. These
marble female figures were carved by America's preeminent
sculptor of the time, Augustus St. Gaudens (1848-1907). He was
paid $60,000 for the sculptures—the largest commission he had
ever received and the last one he completed before his death.
The gleaming, white marble building at 1285 Elmwood Avenue
overlooks Delaware Park Lake, and its dramatic size dominates the
setting. The museum was planned for completion by 1901 for
the Pan-American Exposition, but it did not open until 1905. The
interior is equally impressive with its collection of contemporary
art, one of the finest aggregations of modern painting and
sculpture in America.

Top: The sublime illuminated stained-glass ceiling in the lobby of the Guaranty Building.

Above: Elaborate metalwork on the interior of the Guaranty Building reflects the elaborate design motifs of the exterior.

BUFFALO: GUARANTY BUILDING

Until the 1890s, the only way to build since before the Greeks was wall-supported structures. The taller a structure to be erected, the thicker the walls required. And, therefore, wall thickness became a practical limit for the height of buildings. Then, a breakthrough came by devising steel skeletons that could support a structure to which a thin exterior curtain wall was attached. Now, building height was dramatically increased, and the skyscraper was born. The Guaranty Building at 28 Church Street was built in 1894-1895 and is a milestone in building construction, being one of the first taller buildings in America. It was created by Chicago architect, Louis Henri Sullivan (1856-1924), who was a pioneer in that great American invention, the skyscraper. As cities grew, so did congestion and property values. Owners of office buildings wanted to be in the center of commercial activity, and so it was important to achieve the necessary office space by constructing taller buildings on smaller, expensive lots. Elevators were invented in the 1860s and provided easy access to all the floors. Steel was being mass produced by 1890, and it permitted a strong, slender skeleton that could support the weight of many floors with a light curtain wall for weatherproofing. For Sullivan, it was not enough to build a box that was taller, it had to be aesthetically pleasing. And he was a master at both requirements. With the Guaranty Building, Sullivan made his 13-story box look graceful and soaring. Piers soar uninterrupted past the office floors enhancing the verticality of the structure, which is then capped by a row of oculus windows and a heavy, deep cornice. Red terra-cotta tiles cover the façade in a warm, attractive color, and the tiles are elaborately decorated with Sullivan's signature intricate geometric shapes. The Guaranty Building is so special that it was designated a National Historic Landmark in 1975.

LACKAWANNA: OUR LADY OF VICTORY BASILICA

One of the most spectacular churches in New York State is not in a major city, but in a struggling, middle-class suburb called Lackawanna, which in more halcyon days was home to Bethlehem Steel Company. The church is a jewel and the pride and joy of Lackawanna. The local residents are not alone in their evaluation; the official Vatican newspaper proclaimed Our Lady of Victory one of the most superb churches in America, and Pope Pius XI elevated it to the honors and privileges of a basilica. It is all the result of the remarkable efforts of a young man in the grain and feed business. At age 34, Nelson H. Baker (1842-1936) left his business to become a priest at a failing parish in Lackawanna. Besides his charitable work founding an infant home, a maternity hospital for unwed mothers, and a home and school for tens of thousands of orphan boys, Father Baker inspired his community to donate funds to build a magnificent church dedicated to the Blessed Virgin Mary, Our Lady of Victory. Emile M. Uhlrich of Cleveland, Ohio was the architect, and the chosen style was Italian Renaissance. The exterior of this ornate church, built between 1922 and 1926, is clad in Italian Carrara and Georgian marble. The twin towers are 165 feet high. The great dome has a diameter of 80 feet and a height of 113 feet, among the largest in America. Trumpet-blowing angels that are 18-feet-high stand at the four corners of the dome. The interior was designed by a famous Italian artist, Gonippo Raggi. At the main altar, twisted red Baroque columns of rare Pyrenese marble support a frame around a nine-foot, pure white marble statue of Our Lady of Victory. Father Baker said, "There are a thousand angels in the basilica. Everywhere you look, an angel looks back." And there are 46 varieties of marble from around the world and more than 150 works in stained glass. Solid bronze doors are everywhere, even in back hallways. There is a huge 1981 Delaware organ made in North Tonawanda. The interior is filled with gold leaf, stenciling, and stone statuary. Father Baker himself is buried in the nave amidst the grandeur.

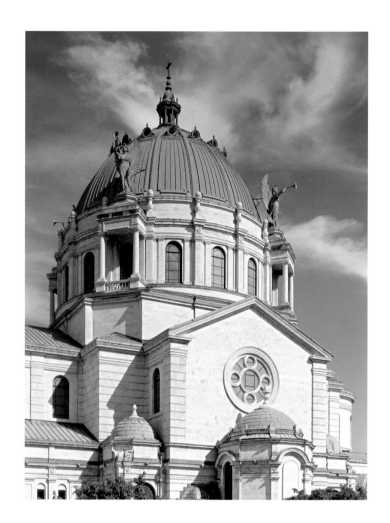

Above: Trumpet-blowing angels are 18 feet tall.

Right: The 14 Stations of the Cross have life-size figures, each station carved from a single block of Italian marble.

Far right: Twisted red Baroque columns of rare Pyrenese marble frame a 9-foot statue of Our Lady of Victory in the domed sanctuary.

OLD FORT NIAGARA

*E*very day, three national flags wave above the parade grounds of Old Fort Niagara, which is located on a peninsula above the Niagara River where it empties into Lake Ontario. Over its 326-year history, the fort has been held by France, Great Britain, and the United States, and the flags symbolize their historic presence. France built the first fortifications in 1679 in order to protect the portage around Niagara Falls, which then offered a water route through the Great Lakes to the vast midwest of the North American continent and to which France laid claim. In 1759, when England fought the French for dominance in North America, the British captured Fort Niagara on July 25. After the American Revolutionary War, the terms of the Treaty of Paris in 1783 drew the boundary line between the United States and Canada, placing the fort in America. England reluctantly, but finally, ceded Fort Niagara to the U.S. in 1794. But the British recaptured the fort in the War of 1812 on December 18, 1813. And again, in the Treaty of Ghent ending the war, the fort was returned to the Americans on May 22, 1815. The oldest and largest building at Fort Niagara is the "French Castle." It is a massive stone structure built in 1726 after the French persuaded the Six Nations of the Iroquois that they were not building a fort, but a "House of Peace" for trading purposes. The result, however, was much more than a trading house. The thick stone walls could resist any armaments of the time; it sheltered a garrison of 60 men; it housed a powder magazine and all the amenities of living quarters, including a well. The top floor had overhanging dormers to allow the French to fire directly down upon an enemy. Finally, it was enclosed by a stockade fence. The French Castle is the oldest building in the area of the Great Lakes.

Top: The massive stone French Castle (in the distance), built in 1726, is the oldest building at Fort Niagara—in fact, it is the oldest structure on the Great Lakes. Part of the South Redoubt is seen at left.

Above: The South Redoubt, seen from the Castle, was built in 1770 and opens directly into the interior of the fort. This blockhouse provided a guard post with cannon on the top floor.

Right: Blue-and-white military uniforms hang in readiness in the Castle for the next parade.

Site Information

- LONG ISLAND

Islip: W. Bayard Cutting Estate, 516-581-1002
www.fordyce.org/long_island/history/Islip

Jones Beach State Park, 516-785-1600
http://nysparks.state.ny.us

Montauk Point Lighthouse, 631-668-2544
www.montauklighthouse.com

Old Westbury: Westbury House, 516-333-0048
www.oldwestburygardens.org

Oyster Bay: Coe Hall, William Robertson Coe Estate
516-922-8600, www.planting fields.org

Oyster Bay: Sagamore Hill, Theodore Roosevelt
House, 516-922-4271, www.nps.gov/sahi/

Sag Harbor: Benjamin Huntting House, 631-725-0770
www.sagharborwhalingmuseum.org

Sag Harbor: Old Customs House, 631-692-4664
Sag Harbor: Old Whalers Church, 631-725-0894
www.sagharborchamber.com/church.htm

- NEW YORK CITY

Brooklyn Botanic Garden, 718-623-7220
www.bbg.org

Brooklyn: Green-Wood Cemetery, 718-768-7300
www.green-wood.com

Ellis Island National Monument, 212-363-3206
www.nps.gov/elis/

Federal Hall National Memorial, 212-825-6888
www.nps.gov/feha/

Morris-Jumel Mansion, 212-923-8008
www.morrisjumel.org

New York Public Library, 212-930-0800
www.nypl.org

- HUDSON RIVER VALLEY

Annandale-on-Hudson: Bard College Performing
Arts Center, 845-758-7950
http://fishercenter.bard.edu

Annandale-on-Hudson: Montgomery Place
845-758-5461
www.hudsonvalley.org

Garrison: Boscobel, 845-265-3638
www.boscobel.org

Greenport: Olana, 518-828-0135
http://nysparks.state.ny.us

Hyde Park: Frederick Vanderbilt Mansion
845-229-9115, www.nps.gov

Kingston: Senate House, 845-338-2786
http://nysparks.state.ny.us

New Paltz: Huguenot Street, 845-255-1660
www.hhs-newpaltz.org

Sleepy Hollow: Philipsburg Manor, 914-631-3992
www.hudsonvalley.org

Tarrytown: Kykuit, Rockefeller Estate, 914-631-8200
www.hudsonvalley.org

Tarrytown: Lyndhurst, 914-631-4481
www.lyndhurst.org

- CAPITAL DISTRICT

Albany: New York State Capitol, 518-474-2418
www.ogs.state.ny.us/

Albany: Schuyler Mansion, 518-434-0834
http://nysparks.state.ny.us

Kinderhook: Lindenwald, Martin Van Buren House
518-758-9689, www.nps.gov/mava

Saratoga Springs: Historical Society, 518-584-6920
www.saratogasprings-historymuseum.org

Saratoga Springs: Lincoln Baths, 518-583-2880

Saratoga Springs: Yaddo, 518-584-0746
www.yaddo.org/

Schenectady: Nott Memorial, Union College
518-388-6000, www.union.edu/Nott/

Schenectady: Schenectady County Historical Society
518-374-0263, www.schist.org

- ADIRONDACKS

Crown Point: Lighthouse/Champlain Memorial
518-597-4666, http://nysparks.state.ny.us

Essex: Belden Noble Memorial Library of Essex
518-963-8079

Essex: Essex Inn, 518-963-8821
www.theessexinn.com/

Newcomb: Camp Santanoni, 518-582-3211
www.newcombny.com/santanoni.htm

North Elba: John Brown Farm, 518-523-3900
http://nysparks.ny.us

Raquette Lake: Camp Sagamore, 315-354-5311
www.sagamore.org/

Ticonderoga: Fort Ticonderoga, 518-585-2821
www.fort-ticonderoga.org

Ticonderoga: Hancock House, 518-585-7868
www.thehancockhouse.org/

Westport Train Station, 518-962-8680
www.depottheatre.org

- MOHAWK RIVER VALLEY

Cooperstown: Farmers' Museum, 607-547-1450
www.farmersmuseum.org

Cooperstown: Fenimore Art Museum, 888-547-1450
www.fenimoreartmuseum.org

Cooperstown Public Library, 814-374-4605
www.cooperstownlibrary.org

Danube: Herkimer Home, 315-823-0398
http://nysparks.state.ny.us

Johnstown: Sir William Johnson Hall, 518-762-8712
http://nysparks.state.ny.us

Oneida: Oneida Community Mansion House
315-363-0745, www.oneidacommunity.org/

Sharon Springs: American Hotel, 518-284-2105
www.americanhotelny.com/

Springfield: Hyde Hall, 607-547-5098
www.hydehall.org

Utica: Fountain Elms, 315-797-0000
www.mwpai.org

Utica: Stanley Theater, 315-724-3854
www.cnyarts.com/stanley/about.php

- THOUSAND ISLANDS

Alexandria Bay: George C. Boldt Castle, 315-482-9724
www.alexbay.org

Clayton: Antique Boat Museum, 315-686-4104
www.abm.org/

Oswego: Fort Ontario, 315-343-4711
http://nysparks.state.ny.us

Oswego: Richardson-Bates House, 315-343-1342
www.oswegony.org

Watertown: Flower Memorial Library, 315-788-2352
www.watertown-ny.gov/flowerlibrary/flowerlibrary.html

Wellesley Island: Thousand Island Park, 315-482-2576

- FINGER LAKES

Auburn: William H. Seward House, 315-252-1283
www.sewardhouse.org/

Bluff Point, Keuka Lake: Garrett Memorial Chapel
315-536-3955

Canandaigua: Granger Homestead, 585-394-1472
www.grangerhomestead.org

Canandaigua: Sonnenberg Mansion and Gardens
585-394-4922, www.sonnenberg.org

Cazenovia: Lorenzo, 315-655-3200
http://nysparks.state.ny.us

Cortland: 1890 House, 607-756-7551
www.1890house.org

Geneva: Rose Hill Mansion, 315-789-3848
www.genevahistoricalsociety.com/

Ithaca: Cornell University, tours of the historic
quadrangle are open to the public

Letchworth State Park: Glen Iris Inn, 585-493-2622
http://www.glenirisinn.com

Syracuse University: Crouse College, the campus
and Crouse College are open to the public

- WESTERN ERIE CANAL

Brockport: Morgan-Manning House, 585-637-3645
Morganmanninghouse@frontiernet.net

Childs: Cobblestone Church and Museum,
585-589-9013, PO Box 363, Albion, NY 14411

Mumford: Genesee Country Village and Museum
585-538-6822, www.gcv.org

Pittsford: Bushnell's Basin, Richardson's Canal House
585-248-5000

Rochester: George Eastman House, 585-271-3361
www.geh.org

Rochester: Memorial Art Gallery, 585-473-7720
http://mag.rochester.edu

Rochester: Susan B. Anthony House, 585-235-6124
www.susanbanthonyhouse.org

- SOUTHERN TIER

Alfred: Celadon Tile Company Office
Alfred University, 607-871-2170, info@alfred.edu

Chautauqua Institution: Athenaeum Hotel
800-821-1881, www.athenaeum-hotel.com

Chautauqua Institution: 800-836-ARTS
www.ciweb.org/

Corning: Corning Museum of Glass, 607-974-8395
www.cmog.org

Elmira: Mark Twain Study, Elmira College
607-735-1869, info@elmira.edu

Johnson City: Sacred Heart Ukrainian Catholic Church
607-797-6293, www.sacredheartucc.org

Westfield: James McClurg House, 716-326-2977
PO Box 7, Westfield, NY 14787

- NIAGARA FRONTIER

Buffalo: Albright-Knox Art Gallery, 716-270-8235
www.albrightknox.org

Buffalo: Darwin D. Martin House, 716-856-3858
www.darwinmartinhouse.org

Buffalo: Forest Lawn Cemetery, 716-885-1600
www.blueskymausoleum.com

Buffalo: Guaranty Building, 716-854-9725
http://freenet.buffalo.edu/bah/a/church/28/

Derby: Graycliff, 716-947-9217
http://graycliff.bfn.org/

East Aurora: Roycroft Inn, 716-652-4735
www.roycroftinn.com

Lackawanna: Our Lady of Victory Basilica
716-828-9444, www.ourladyofvictory.org

Old Fort Niagara: 716-745-7611
http://nysparks.state.ny.us

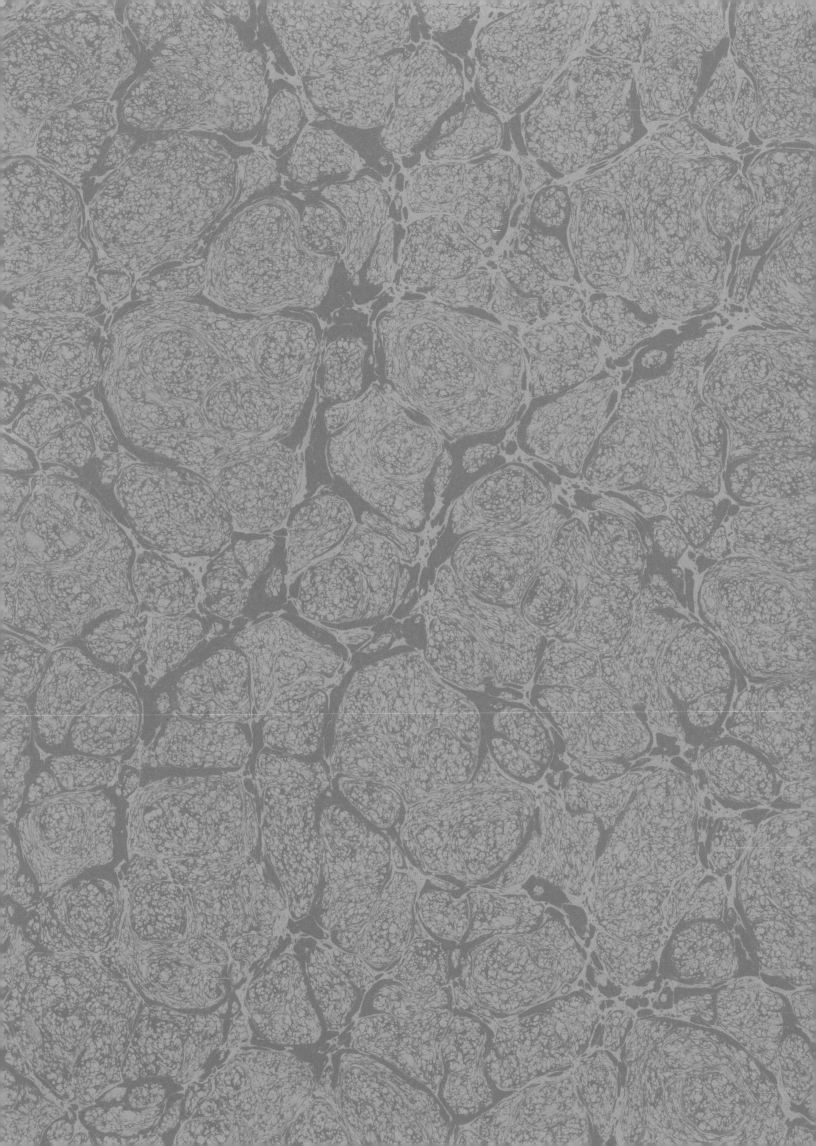